The Cosmic Romance with Existence

A Personal Guide Book for Spiritual Warriors to Merge Their Light with The Cosmic Light

MURALI DHARAN

PARTRIDGE

Library of Congress Control Number: 2022903410
ISBN: Hardcover 978-1-4828-7937-7
Softcover 978-1-4828-7936-0
eBook 978-1-5437-6912-8

Print information available on the last page.

To order additional copies of this book, contact
Toll Free +65 3165 7531 (Singapore)
Toll Free +60 3 3099 4412 (Malaysia)
orders.singapore@partridgepublishing.com

www.partridgepublishing.com/singapore

I dedicate this book with gratitude and reverence
to the beautiful divine existence (universe)
and to my spiritual masters who have
guided me in my spiritual path

CONTENTS

PREFACE

My inspiration to write arose after I received an intuitive call to contribute to humanity and existence. This inspiration rose through a profoundly intimate and intuitive relationship formed with existence through daily meditative practice.

My work involves the healing of the minds, emotions, and unfavorable situations of humans, and it has been another source of inspiration. I hold a bachelor's degree with a post-graduate dip in counseling and a master's in social work, specializing in couples and family therapy. I have more than a decade of experience providing human services. In this decade of experience, I realized that both the professional worker and the client need support and stability in the provision of human services. Being in a clinical position that includes healing, I realized that besides theoretical and empirical knowledge, good qualities of consciousness are crucial to providing impeccable interventions.

I have also been practicing raja yoga, kriya yoga, and various meditation methods for more than fifteen years. My empirical knowledge in martial arts, meditation, and yoga has helped me understand how mental and physical fitness play vital roles in spiritual development. I have been able to integrate and create sagacious methods for spiritual well-being and development that can benefit humanity.

I have learned that a healer suffering from his own unhealed pains and lacking adequate self-knowledge and self-healing abilities might end up causing pain to others. To become excellent therapeutic healers, healers should be wary and conscious of their own pains hindering the healing process for others. This book is meant to share spiritual guidance for raising consciousness and healing humanity.

The purpose of this book is to help readers work on themselves and to inspire them to help others. When this book is read consciously, readers will build a loving and trusting relationship with existence, which in turn helps them realize their life's purpose, raise their consciousness, and self-heal from pains and suffering within a strong intimate relationship with existence.

The concept of "existence" in this book refers to the universe (God, higher powers or divine powers). A robust intimate relationship with existence is imperative for raising consciousness and gaining self-realization. As our consciousness rises, it emancipates us from pains and suffering. The book subtly emphasizes the nonduality between man (who lives in existence) and God (as existence). In other words, the creator (God) lives within the creation (man). The aim of the book is also to help man to realize the nondual relationship between man and God. Realizing oneself means realizing the God within; realizing the supreme truth (that God is within) frees one from pains and suffering in life.

I have integrated experiences and knowledge gained from meditations, spiritual and life lessons, and musings from existence into this book. Every chapter was written after an hour of meditation to ensure that the words are consciously chosen and expressed to meet the audience's needs. My goal has been to write in a simple, comprehensible, and organized manner to delight and guide readers. I hope this book will be an immense benefit for anyone working on their spiritual growth.

To use this book effectively, five important sublime qualities are needed: love, trust, courage, will, and discipline. One must love life, love existence, and have a strong love for oneself. The second quality is building a sturdy trust between oneself and existence. The third quality is the courage to dive deep into oneself to understand purpose in life, consciousness, and liberation. Above all, one should have the will to learn and the discipline to put to regular practice what has been learned.

This spiritual guidebook will help you merge your light with the cosmic light and be a light to yourself and others. My thanks to existence and humanity. Enjoy reading!

CHAPTER 1

The Heaven and Hell within Us

"Existence" is what I call the universe. Existence holds the general powers of creation, manifestation, and dissolution. As humans, we see ourselves as an element of existence. We tell ourselves, "I am a human, and I am part of this existence."

As we become more meditative and aware, we realize that not only are we an element of existence, but we *are* existence. To arrive at this point of self-realization, we have to work on ourselves. Working on ourselves requires deep, profound self-reflections, meditations, and self-healings to raise our consciousness. Self-realization is a complex concept to grasp. It takes some time to experience and comprehend the true meaning, but as you read further, you will be able to capture the gist of these esoteric insights.

Two types of energies manifest within us and the existence: one is divine, and the other is demonic. The divine energy is our consciousness, and the demonic energy is our unconsciousness. Another way to put this is, heaven is consciousness, and hell is unconsciousness. Our unconsciousness leads us into suffering, and our consciousness rescues us from suffering. If we scout deeper, we will realize that we are responsible for our heaven and hell.

COMMUNICATION METHODS OF EXISTENCE

The existence communicates with us using various methods and modes. There are two types of messages or signals from the existence, internal and external signals. To study internal signals, we have to check on ourselves. For example, if we have terrible hangovers (headaches) due to excessive drinking, we know that alcohol and our lack of consciousness for our health is the cause. A hangover headache is an *internal* communication signal stating that a harmful substance has entered our body.

How about environments or relationships that exhaust us and give us problems? These are the existence's *external* communication signals telling us to be wary of unpleasant people and situations. These signals also hint to us to deal consciously with relationships and environments that drag us into unconsciousness.

When receiving messages from existence, we have to look into options and situations within and beyond our control. The existence usually alerts us with messages and then gives us the freedom of choice to make our decisions.

If we cannot decipher the existence's messages clearly, and we continue acting in ways that don't help with the growth of our consciousness, it will lead us to more pain and suffering. Messages or lessons from the existence will be repeated until we take appropriate actions for our positive growth and spiritual development.

When I was trapped in intense pain and suffering arising from my ignorance, I was utterly perplexed about why my life was extremely miserable. However, through profound self-reflections and meditations, I realized that the existence was trying to communicate with me.

In the beginning, my ignorance caused me to dismiss the existence's messages. Then I learned one important lesson: the existence is communicating with everyone daily. But many of us cannot comprehend the existence's messages, as we aren't aligned with the cosmic energies of existence. As we become more aligned with the cosmic energies of the existence, we gradually eschew ignorance; we will develop the ability to decipher and comprehend messages from the existence.

The existence is communicating with us daily. Only through wakefulness can we sense the messages clearly and make our lives better.

CHAPTER 2

THE GENERAL POWERS OF EXISTENCE

I LEARNED FROM MY SPIRITUAL INSIGHTS that existence possesses several types of powers. One of the great ways to experience and taste these succulent powers of existence is to meditate. I will share what I have experienced and learned about them.

Through meditations, I was able to build a deep and intimate relationship with existence. This relationship with existence helped me to grow my creative energies as a writer. That is one of the reasons I am writing this book.

Moreover, meditation helped me to break away from habits of smoking and drinking. I was a compulsive smoker and drinker who was constantly worried about my actions. Each time I tried hard to stop smoking and drinking, I would relapse within weeks. I reached a point of frustration where I told myself that I would never give up this habit. Eventually, I gave up trying to quit these habits.

All I can remember is suddenly losing my temptations to smoke and drink. To this day, it puzzles me when I recall how I managed to quit. There were no struggles or arduous efforts on my part to quit my bad habits—except being consistent with my daily meditations. I know that some higher powers were supporting me in my recovery. These higher forces were none other than the powers of existence.

If you were to ask me whether it is possible to quit smoking and drinking without making relentless efforts, I would say it is possible by building a deep intimate relationship with existence.

Let me share three general powers of existence: creation, manifestation, and dissolution.

CREATION

Existence holds the powers of creation, and the creative powers of existence are phenomenal. Procreation is a known quality of existence. Every living being in existence procreates. These are the body's creative qualities.

THE FIVE CREATIVE ELEMENTS OF EXISTENCE IN THE HUMAN BODY

Existence is created with the presence of five elements: air, water, space/sky, earth, and fire. Humans hold the same five elements in their bodies. Metaphysically, the earth represents the body or flesh, fire represents the heat energy in the human body, water represents blood, and air is the life force that we breathe. Sky or space is the consciousness that lies beyond our mind and the body. There is something special about space, as it serves as a point of transcendence into higher consciousness. This space is known as the "thoughtless center."

Let me explain more about space. It can be best experienced through awareness and mindfulness. By being constantly watchful over our thoughts, we will sporadically enter into space—a gap or distance between one thought to the other. Space is also the entry point to a thoughtless state, superconsciousness, and cosmic consciousness.

Meditation methods work on stilling our minds and bringing us into the present moment. As our minds become still and no longer wander into the past or future, we enter space. Transcending into cosmic consciousness helps us to realize ourselves and our oneness with existence.

TWO TYPES OF CREATIVITY GRANTED BY EXISTENCE

Existence grants two types of creativity.

- **Procreativity** is reproduction or sexual energy.
- **Creativity** is the quality of higher consciousness, sexual energy that rises and transforms to serve higher purposes.

The element of space holds many qualities of higher consciousness. One of those qualities is creativity. Creativity is beyond the quality of the mind and body. Mind and body are only tools that express creativity. Creativity is a quality born of space. For example, water (creativity) comes out from a faucet (mind and body), but the water doesn't belong to the faucet.

Every human has the power of creativity in them. This is a gift from existence. Our power of creativity gets enhanced with a close and intimate relationship with existence. For example, if one meditates by keeping the mind still for a few minutes daily, the powers of creativity grow.

We can understand the creative powers of existence, but understanding how existence was created is an esoteric and unfathomed truth.

MANIFESTATION

Manifestation is a commonly discussed topic. I would say manifestation is simply communication with existence. As we talk to the existence, existence responds. I will share five methods you can use as guidelines to make your manifestations work better.

1. **Meditate first.** When it comes to communicating with existence, it is good to speak after meditation. The purpose of meditation is to clear the noises in our minds and calm ourselves down before speaking. We can communicate clearly and positively to existence when we are calm and relaxed.
2. **Use clear messages.** Do not send complicated messages. The existence communicates using energy waves. We want to ensure that these energy waves travel smoothly and not in a chaotic manner. We can either speak aloud and clearly to the existence or communicate from our subconscious mind. For example, we can close our eyes, go deep into our subconscious, and then visualize or express our wishes to the existence.
3. **Express gratitude.** The magic key to successful communication is gratitude. Expressing gratitude to the existence will make the existence respond with an abundance of positivity to us.
4. **Be positive.** Always speak positively and ask for positive things. The existence communicates using energy waves. Never send hate messages to the existence. For example, never pray for negative things to happen. When we are angry, we tend to send aggressive messages to the existence. These aggressive and unconscious messages

create stormy energy waves that don't travel in a smooth direction. Negative messages host negative energies and react negatively. If we send negativity to others, we will receive negativity back. It is like a ball that we throw to the wall. The ball bounces back to us. So be conscious of what you speak. Every word you communicate holds a form of energy vibration.

5. **Act beneficially.** Contribute to the existence by actions that benefit the existence and the lives that are in existence. For example, helping the poor, preserving nature, and feeding hungry animals. The existence reciprocates with an abundance of goodness for your actions.

What if someone causes me harm?

Remember that existence naturally knows how to advocate for your justice if someone has caused harm to you and you are in pain. Therefore, never manifest hatred for your enemies and raise the negative frequencies in your manifestations. Always remain conscious, calm, and lucid in your communication with existence.

HEALING POWERS

Another part of manifestation is working with the healing energies of existence. It is about drawing healing energies from existence to self-heal and heal others. However, this requires deep learning and proper practice. Let me share a simple three-step self-healing method.

1. **Grounding exercise.** It is good to meditate before doing any healing actions. With a clear and stable mind,

our communications with existence will also be clear and stable.

2. **Drawing energy from existence.** Close your eyes, place your hands near your heart, and visualize light energy from existence entering into the pain areas of your body. Imagine and feel the warmness of this light.
3. **Affirmation.** Use affirmative healing words when healing those areas of pain. For example, you could say, "I am healing, I am better, and I can feel the pain leaving my body."

This practice has to be done regularly with trust and faith. Healing is a gradual process and not an overnight miracle. If you are on medication, it is good to practice healing while still being medically compliant, as spiritual healing takes time.

Blessings and Protective Powers

Existence blesses during prayers, meditation, and any spiritual practices. These blessings protect us in times of challenging and risky situations. You can experience the blessings and protection of existence if you have raised your spiritual frequencies and vibrations. The ways and methods used by existence to provide blessings and protection are infinite. For example, some may have faced life-threatening situations where they were saved miraculously. There are times when existence reveals its powers, and there are also times when it conceals. Regardless of how existence expresses itself to us, we can be assured that the existence will never let down the faith, trust and love we have for it. The existence reciprocates with goodness for all positive efforts and conscious actions that are aligned to its cosmic energies.

Psychic Powers

You may ask what psychic powers are. These are also powers drawn from existence. There are various methods and practices to attain them. To understand psychic energies, we have to be aware that both allied and opposing forces reside in existence. Allied forces are positive energies, and opposing forces are negative energies. Psychic work requires understanding that the divine energies and the demonic energies are like dual sides of a coin (existence).

Psychic energies develop through meditation and different types of spiritual practices. These practices are done together with faith and trustful communication with existence.

A well-known psychic practice is the activation of the third eye. The third eye is activated and energized when we center our attention at the midpoint between the eyebrows during meditation, thus raising our ability to see and know things beyond the physical dimension.

Dissolution

The third general power of existence is dissolution. Dissolution is existence's ability to break, subdue, and transform. Dissolution is never wholly a negative term. Every beginning has an ending. For example, birth and death are creation and dissolution processes in existence. Birth is the creative part, and death is the dissolution. Dissolution processes are imperative for us to raise our consciousness.

Breaking Away and Letting Go

We break away from pains and suffering when we raise our consciousness. We are relieved from the vicious cycles of pains and suffering as we raise our consciousness. Pains and suffering are messages that trigger us to awaken our consciousness. For example, letting go of a thought, emotion, communication, action, environment, habit, or a sinful lifestyle to raise our consciousness are all acts of dissolution.

TRANSFORMATION OF ENERGY

Sexual energy is spiritual energy. If sexual energies are being channeled in the right direction instead of being dissipated, it will help raise the consciousness. Examples of the dissipation of energies include excessive masturbation, addiction to pornography, and engaging in perverse activities.

Breaking away from dissipative actions and transforming energies for a constructive purpose is dissolution. If these sexual energies are transformed to higher planes, it helps raise consciousness and enhance creativity and healing powers. Similarly, other energies such as sadness, anger, and any form of pain and suffering can be transformed instead of being released from the wrong pores.

The greatest power one can relish
is the power of existence that showers within oneself.

CHAPTER 3

CONSCIOUSNESS AND SATORI

DURING MY MEDITATION PRACTICE, THE more I practiced being aware, the more I started witnessing glimpses of golden light. In the beginning, I didn't know what the golden light in my meditative vision was. When I shared my experience with a group of enlightened spiritual masters, I was taught that this experience is called *satori*. Satori is a mini enlightening experience where we sporadically witness our consciousness.

KNOWING CONSCIOUSNESS

Consciousness means total awareness. Consciousness holds the collective information of yourself. Consciousness is our inner state of being, which lies beyond the mind and the body. How we perceive messages in existence reflects our inner state of consciousness. The term *consciousness* means the true self. It is about entering into the space of self-realization.

Let me explain about consciousness. Consciousness is separate from the mind and body, but it permeates into the mind and body. Consciousness is an inner light shed onto the mind and the body. Let's say a book is our body, and the pages inside the book are our mind (thoughts); we need the light energy to permeate the book and its pages so that we can see and read it. Similarly, this light energy inside us is consciousness, and it permeates into our body (book) and mind (pages).

Though the book and the pages remain separate from the light energy, light energy is still needed to see the book and read the pages. Without light, we will not be able to see or read the book. Likewise, we need our consciousness for the functioning of the mind and body. If we raise the brightness of the light, the words on the pages will appear sharp and clear. Similarly, as our consciousness gets raised, we gain clear perceptions and clairvoyance, and we function better as humans.

There are two realms of consciousness. They are lower and higher realms of consciousness. In the lower realms, we face unconsciousness. Unconsciousness is the cause of our pains and suffering. Higher realms are the states in which we radiate compassion, love, gratitude, contentment, and other constructive, positive qualities. These qualities help us in our worldly and spiritual development. We will look into the stages of consciousness in chapter 10.

On the path toward self-realization,
we first come to taste a drop of water,
and later we realize we are inside the ocean.

CHAPTER 4

Common Methods to Raise Consciousness

There are many ways to transcend into a state of consciousness. Some common ways are doing deep self-reflections (introspection), being in the present moment, meditating and praying. Though they sound easy and the practice appears simple, doing them requires a tremendous amount of discipline and effort.

From my personal experience, I have realized that the best way to do self-reflections and gain a profound understanding of myself is to do self-reflections after an hour of meditation. I find that meditation is like a torchlight. It shines on my dark sides and makes me aware of every corner that needs healing and change. Therefore, after meditations, I could spot my unhealed areas easily when I do my self-reflections. I realized that an unhealthy mind and body aren't supportive peers when it comes to raising our consciousness. Growing our consciousness involves keeping our minds and bodies healthy.

SELF-REFLECTIONS

Deep self-reflection means checking on our thoughts, emotions, communication, and actions. This method raises our sense of self-awareness. Deep self-reflection is also known as *introspection*. In this process of introspection, parts of our mind check on other parts of our mind. For instance, if I reflected on my argument with my friend yesterday, I will ask reflective questions such as, "Why did I speak in this way? What caused me to argue?" This process helps me uncover more profound truths about myself. This is an effective method to understand oneself, but it is arduous to reach a superconsciousness state.

THE EGO

When we do self-reflection, we explore ourselves in every layer. The final point of all self-reflection is arriving at an understanding of our ego. If we apply brutal honesty to self-reflective sessions, we will come to a truthful answer. As we study our answers, we will realize that almost every answer is tied to our ego. Therefore, the ultimate purpose of self-reflection is to reveal our ego and its functioning.

When we reach the state of self-realization, our ego drops. The ego is never totally wrong. A healthy ego is essential in saving our self-respect and working towards positive progress. We should be aware that the unhealthy parts of the ego are the ones that contribute to pains and suffering.

BEING IN THE PRESENT MOMENT

Another effective method is keeping the mind in the present moment. Being in the present means a person remains aware, conscious and watchful of his thoughts, emotions, communication, and actions every moment. Conscious actions gradually lead us into the state of understanding the supreme truth. How does this happen?

Bringing the mind to the present moment limits the wavering of the mind into the past and future. The present moment stills and stabilizes the mind. To reach consciousness, we have to reach a state of the thoughtless moment—no mind. Thoughtless moments are attained only when the mind stabilizes and stops wandering into the past and future.

MEDITATING

Meditating is so far the best method to bring our minds into the present moment. Meditations help us to arrive into a thoughtless state and bring us into a state of superconsciousness and cosmic consciousness. Meditation is charging ourselves with the cosmic energy waves of existence. These waves are the driving forces to attain self-realization.

PRAYERS

Prayers help us to express gratitude, manifest solutions, and create an aura of protection. Prayers are messages sent out to the existence. Prayers are helpful to stabilize the mind. It helps a person to feel relief after speaking to the existence. It is good to supplement spiritual practices with prayers, self-reflections, meditations, and conscious actions to achieve the maximum spiritual benefits from existence.

Raising Spiritual Frequencies

Spiritual frequencies are like an individual point system in spirituality. The higher your points, the closer you are to existence. The purpose of a close and intimate relationship with existence is to dissolve pains and suffering and achieve self-realization. Honest self-reflections, conscious actions, meditations, and prayers raise spiritual frequencies.

As your spiritual frequencies rise, your communication with existence becomes smoother, and you gradually develop an inviolable ability to comprehend the crux and depth of heavenly messages.

CHAPTER 5

Awareness Is the First Door

During my first year as a student of the degree program in counseling, I learned the first module about self-awareness. Today I have realized very deeply that self-awareness is not only necessary to understand ourselves and help others; it is the first door to open when it comes to attaining superconsciousness and creating oneness with existence.

Awareness means watchfulness, alertness, and self-knowing. It is about being alive and present. Knowing briefly about our thoughts, emotions, communication, and actions and letting our thoughts wander in the past and future is never defined as awareness. There is a difference between simply knowing and being completely aware.

An example of non-awareness would be thinking of my work, an upcoming wedding event, or a painful experience when having my dinner; I only know that I am eating, but I am not present in the here and now when I am eating.

Most times, we know only the tip of the iceberg in understanding thoughts, emotions, communication, and actions. Let me explain awareness and how it helps to achieve higher consciousness.

THE BRUTAL TRUTH

We must be completely aware of the brutal truth of our own thoughts, emotions, communication, and actions. We need to know every deep layer of the truths about ourselves. We can arrive at this stage if we are completely honest with ourselves. We can achieve this honesty by letting go of our own biases and ego during self-reflections.

I work on accepting my errors, and I make no excuses or reasons to cover and justify those errors during reflections. For example, I smoked a cigarette not because my dad was a smoker or my peers influenced me, but because I enjoyed it. I become honest and take responsibility for myself. Be honest to yourself first, and then your honesty itself will help you discard the thoughts, emotions, communication, and actions that cause you suffering and pain.

PRESENT MOMENT AND CONSCIOUS ACTIONS

Being completely present means we are in the here and now of our actions. We become completely aware, conscious, and watchful over our thoughts, emotions, communication, and actions in the present moment.

When we say a person is conscious, we mean that the person is completely aware of their thoughts, emotions, communication, and actions. Conscious people always have a sense of quality in their actions because of awareness.

As we are working towards higher consciousness, we should practice being as conscious as possible. Conscious action builds more stability and stillness in our minds. It prevents a wandering mind that harbors intrusive and anxious thoughts. Stillness and stability of mind are needed for transcending into the higher state of consciousness. If we become aware and conscious of our actions, we become more awake and more alive.

Personally, I find being in the present moment to be the most challenging action for me. I am sure most of us will feel the same. Though we cannot be completely present, it is good to be as present as possible. To practice this, we must be more watchful over our present thoughts, emotions, communication, and actions from moment to moment.

WHO AM I?

The question "Who am I?" will help you begin your inward journey. Ask yourself constantly, "Who am I, and what is my purpose?" These questions give you a glimpse of consciousness and turn your vision inwards. Inward vision is the gateway to higher consciousness and self-realization. Inward vision awakens us from our metaphysical sleep. These questions exert a magnetic pull towards your inner light.

To travel smoothly in all parts of life,
the very first place to visit is yourself.

CHAPTER 6

WHAT IS UNCONSCIOUSNESS?

I HAVE HEARD ABOUT DEMONS AND angels. To me, the most dangerous demon is my sense of unconsciousness. I limited myself from externalizing problems and started working on myself. I believe the best spiritual cleansing is the one done to myself in overcoming my inner demons of unconsciousness. My inner demons are the leading cause of my suffering and pain.

ACTS OF UNCONSCIOUSNESS

Have you ever come across a colleague whose jokes always hover around sex? Or a man who controls his anger and frustrations around his boss and then later goes home and vents his anger onto his family? When being drawn into deep thoughts, a smoker might not know how many cigarettes he has smoked. Someone is liked because of how the person looks, but the deep underlying reasons for liking the person may be unknown. A man looks at a beautiful woman on the train but can't recall admiring her when he reaches home. All these are acts of unconsciousness.

Being drawn into the past and future and being unaware of the present are acts of unconsciousness. Acting without knowing the root cause of our thoughts, emotions, communication, and actions are also unconscious states. Unconsciousness means expressing our thoughts and feelings in an innately unclear manner and not being aware of ego-driven actions.

Being in a state of unconsciousness is also known as a metaphysical sleep or spiritual ignorance. A person's biases, distorted perceptions, rigid thinking patterns, and negative emotions tied to the ego cause unconsciousness to surface. Unconsciousness is the cause of many pains and suffering in a person's life. Unconsciousness causes us to act and function while being under the control of the ego.

Suppression and Repression

When we suppress or repress a thought, the thought multiplies and causes painful impacts on us. Suppression and repression are an unconscious using of force on ourselves. When we are told not to think about something, we will think about it more—this is how our mind works. These actions in our minds are acts of unconsciousness. When thoughts and emotions are suppressed or repressed without being properly addressed and transformed, they return in the form of ungrounded aggressions, passive behaviors, perversion, and other unhealthy forms of actions that are destructive to the well-being of humanity.

If we can conquer the demons within us, we never have to be afraid of the demons around us.

CHAPTER 7

METAPHYSICAL SLEEP

I HAVE REALIZED THAT FROM MOMENT to moment, if I remain in a metaphysical sleep, I am passing the responsibility to my inner unconscious demons to run my life. The question is not about me, living my life. It is the question of whether I am alive. Being alive means being completely self-aware.

As we lose our conscious wakefulness, we are said to be in a metaphysical sleep. We remain unconscious about how our thoughts, emotions, communication, and actions adversely affect ourselves and others around us. Lacking mindfulness, remaining ignorant about the unconscious parts inside us, and not taking action towards positive changes produce a metaphysical sleep. Metaphysical sleep is usually caused by lacking a clear sense of self-awareness and profound reflective skills.

All of us have unconscious issues. We heal and clear these unconscious issues as we work towards knowing about ourselves. It is crucial to identify these issues and prevent them from hindering personal growth and well-being. Through meditations and profound self-reflection, we can see our sense of unconsciousness. Meditation also develops our ability to spot and sense the unconsciousness in others.

Being in a prolonged state of metaphysical sleep leads us to face many life challenges. Problems repeat themselves again and again until we wake up from this metaphysical sleep. When a problem occurs, we avoid it, we complain, or we use the same unconscious methods to manage it, but this will cause the problem to reoccur in our lives. Sometimes, these problems become more painful and worse.

Pain is the existence's way of communicating and alerting us. The existence uses pain to help us understand that we need to change our approach to handling problems. Changing our approach means simply being more awake and conscious when dealing with a situation. If there were no pain, many of us would remain in our unconscious comfort zone of repeating our errors.

We might face challenges progressing if we continue remaining in a metaphysical sleep. Only awakening brings us towards self-realization. In the next chapter, we will see how metaphysical sleep affects our daily living.

Metaphysical sleep is the hometown for pains and suffering.

CHAPTER 8

METAPHYSICAL SLEEP CAUSES PAINS AND SUFFERING

LET US LOOK AT THE challenges that contribute to the pains and suffering of humanity due to metaphysical sleep. We can refer to this list to be aware of how parts of unconsciousness in us have caused intense pain and suffering in our lives. These are just guidelines—the list may not be applicable for those suffering from severe mental illness. If one is suffering from mental illness, it is good to seek treatments while simultaneously working on personal and spiritual growth.

I gathered this information through my empirical knowledge. When I become aware of how these unconscious issues control me, I immediately repair them. I express my gratitude for the daily practice of meditations. Without meditations, I wouldn't be able to decipher what the existence wants to tell me about my unconscious issues and how the existence plans to rescue me towards wakefulness.

I would say these areas aren't flaws but areas that need healing to help one transcend to higher levels of consciousness.

From my experience, I would say these areas can be healed with the consistent practice of meditation.

You may refer to this list to check whether these conditions of metaphysical sleep contribute to any pain and suffering and then gradually work on healing them.

- having biases
- having perceptions clouded by intrapersonal issues—biases, ego, or any ungrounded thoughts and emotions that interfere with perception
- suppressing thoughts and emotions
- exhibiting violent, aggressive or bullying behaviors arising from issues of power and control
- imposing values and beliefs on others
- lacking sensitivity for self and others
- lacking emotional intelligence and empathetic intelligence
- applying rigid thinking patterns (for example, functioning more like a robot in daily life activities)
- using half-baked knowledge to evaluate situations
- arriving at "dead sure" conclusions (the less I know, the more rigidly I know it)
- externalizing blame or self-blaming
- consistently making excuses for not taking any actions towards positive changes
- relying heavily on the opinions of others or having difficulty thinking for oneself and liking to follow what others say; that is, the puppet or follower mindset
- being overly materialistic and enslaved to worldly pleasures; running after luxury materials throughout life and forgetting the purpose of one's birth
- constantly finding fault in people and engaging in harmful communications that arise out of negative

thoughts and emotions; for example, degrading others to make oneself feel better
- avoiding challenges and confrontations most times
- having standby rationalizations to mask actions and ego; or example, saying "I hit you because I care about you" or "I drank alcohol to drown my worries"
- facing addictions
- functioning under the control of one's own ego
- living with a victim mindset
- having positive thinking habits that are toxic; for example, desperately finding positivity in every situation
- having habitually negative thoughts; for example, finding problems in every solution
- being unconsciously addicted to suffering and pain; for example, leaving an exhausting work environment but finding a new job in a similar environment, or leaving an abusive partner and getting attached to a new partner who has the same negative traits
- constantly seeking validation, unable to accept painful truths about oneself

Here are some other conditions of metaphysical sleep:

- spiritual bypassing (see chapter 32)
- confidence issues, self-esteem issues, fear in taking calculated risks or unconsciously being trapped in a comfort zone
- overly submissive behavior
- overly dominant behavior
- poor sense of self-reflection, such as biased reflections
- poor communication skills

To explore a couple of these, if I fear taking a calculated risk, I may not resign from a company even if I don't like my unfair employer because my pay is high and it is risky to explore other options. I may have many rationalizations ("sensible" excuses) to back up my decision not to take action. Often, people are unaware of how their unconscious issues affect their life decisions.

If a communication goes well, that does not always mean that the other party truly understands your point of view. They may gladly accept your points unless it pacifies their own unconscious issues. They will agree with you only if your story fits their narratives. In other words, you must feed their biases and beliefs to score points from them or to be in their good books. This is also in a way, an unconscious form of communication.

Look out for any intrapersonal and interpersonal issues that contribute to suffering and pain. Pain and suffering are existence's messages to us that we are not aligned with the cosmic energies of existence. It is through these pains and suffering that we awaken and heal. Awakening means we work on conscious ways to align ourselves to the cosmic energies of existence. Aligning ourselves with the energies of existence leads us to heal and enter into a more profound awakening stage that gradually unshackles us from pain and suffering, leading us to self-realization and complete freedom. We will understand that pain and suffering play crucial and high-yielding roles in our lives if we can comprehend their meanings with wakefulness.

Lessons from existence will be repeated, causing us pains and suffering until we work on them consciously.

CHAPTER 9

WHY AM I TRAPPED IN A METAPHYSICAL SLEEP?

THESE ARE SEVERAL REASONS PEOPLE are still in metaphysical sleep. With my empirical knowledge, I found these to be the areas where you may locate agents contributing in negative ways to a long metaphysical sleep.

AWARENESS

- **Do self-reflections correctly.** Lack of brutal honesty towards oneself is the cause of poor self-reflections. Self-reflections aren't done by just peeling the first two layers of the potatoes to make potato chips!
- **Practice meditation or meditating correctly**. Incorrect meditation happens when eyes are closed and the mind is thinking of other things (closed-eye daydreaming) and not meditating.
- **Be aware of your own spiritual blockages**. These are called chakra blockages.

- **Be aware of how your ego controls you.** For example, thinking that I am always greater and better than someone else and looking down on others.
- **Stop adding rationalizations to your actions to fit your narrative.** For example, "I watched porn to keep me happy, and it helps me to cope with life problems. It doesn't affect my daily functioning. So, it's fine."

LIFESTYLE

- **Disentangle yourself from a mechanical life.** A mechanical lifestyle never allows you to have proper time management for introspection. Let's say that I work from 8 a.m. to 11 p.m., and then I come home, shower, watch TV, and sleep … and the next day I repeat the same routine. That's a mechanical life.
- **Disentangle yourself from addictive cycles.** People drink, smoke, and indulge in other unhealthy activities that help them escape reality. A substance abuser rationalizes these addictive habits as coping behaviors.

VISION

- **Invest your energy more in self-inquiry and less in the affairs of others.** Some people spend most of their time checking on the lives of others and talking about others: "I like digging the garden of my neighbor to look for treasures and forget all about planting my seeds in my garden."
- **Work towards becoming a better person.** You get better day by day by improving your mental and physical

fitness and positive actions. Never compare yourself with others but consistently evaluate your progress in growing your sense of self-awareness, character and intelligence.

To awaken from a metaphysical sleep,
we have to realize and admit our
spiritual ignorance to ourselves.

CHAPTER 10

The Stages of Consciousness

I WILL USE A PYRAMID TO describe the stages of consciousness. This pyramid is like a rank system in spiritual development. The higher you climb, the more insight, intuition, clarity and wisdom you gain, and suffering gradually ceases. The ranks in the spiritual world are different from the ranks in the material world. The broad base of the pyramid symbolizes too many desires, expectations, negative thoughts and feelings, and insecurities. The top of the pyramid represents the sharpness of intelligence and the steady rising to the higher self.

Think of consciousness as having the form of a pyramid reaching a peak. At the lower realms of the pyramid are these stages of consciousness:

1. **cosmic unconsciousness** or complete unawareness
2. **collective unconscious mind**, the collective unawareness that leads to suffering and pain
3. **unconscious mind**, the individual unawareness leads to suffering and pain

The stages of consciousness at higher realms of the pyramid are:

4. **conscious mind**, the mind that functions in the present moment
5. **conscious no-mind**, the state of thoughtlessness
6. **superconsciousness**, the state of self-realization and oneness with true self as your light unites with the Divine Light, and your light of consciousness merges with the light of existence
7. **cosmic consciousness**, the state of realizing your oneness with existence or the universe

In *cosmic unconsciousness* (stage 1), we are unaware that we are one with the universe.

The *collective unconscious mind* (stage 2) describes the environment in which a person faces unconscious moments. It could be a family or work environment where collective suffering and pain occurs, or it could be about belonging to a particular group in which thoughts, emotions, communication, and actions are delivered in similar unconscious frequencies.

The *unconscious mind* (stage 3) describes the mind of the individual who goes through pain and suffering. The unconscious mind is the exit point for expressions that flow out of the lower realms of consciousness. For example, ungrounded aggressions or any other troubling thoughts, emotions, communication, and actions are released here.

The *conscious mind* (stage 4), as we start to enter the higher realms, is the state of being in the here and now. It is being in the present moment. The conscious mind is the exit point for any expressions that flow out from the higher state of consciousness. For example, feelings of love and compassion are expressed here.

The *conscious no-mind* (stage 5) is the state of thoughtlessness—the point where our thoughts stop when we meditate consistently. We enter into this state sporadically during meditation. For example, there is space between one thought and another thought. These spaces are entry points to higher consciousness.

The state of *superconsciousness* (stage 6) is the state of self-realization. It is known as the state of oneness with self, non-duality (I am one with the Supreme Being), union with the higher powers, or merging with the supreme truth.

Cosmic consciousness (stage 7) is the highest state, where we realize the truth that we are one with existence or universe.

WHAT IS THE SUBCONSCIOUS MIND?

The mind itself is a phenomenal dimension. One part of our mind is the subconscious mind. The subconscious mind holds information and memories that do not appear on the surface of our conscious mind but act more like "backstage performers." The subconscious mind is a vital aspect of the mind. Any information held in our subconscious mind will affect our overall functioning as humans.

Think of learning to drive. When we first learn to drive, we learn it consciously. After driving for some years, we drive mechanically. By "mechanically," I mean that our minds can think about other things while driving, yet we still drive correctly to our desired destination. Our subconscious mind assists us to drive correctly even when we aren't fully present in our conscious mind while driving.

The subconscious mind acts as one of the communication platforms between us and existence. Through deep meditative practices, we can develop the ability to send and receive messages from existence through our subconscious minds.

The subconscious mind has many purposes. It holds information that arises from unconsciousness and consciousness. For example, my suppressed desires are hidden in my subconscious mind and may appear in my dreams. At the same time, my conscious affirmations are also banked into my subconscious mind. For example, when I consciously say, "I am healing," this message also goes into my subconscious mind and helps me with the healing process.

When existence wants to send me a message, it may deposit messages into my subconscious mind too. So we must be aware that the subconscious mind acts like our very own giant letterbox. Meditation also helps us to comprehend and decipher our subconscious messages.

Raising consciousness is like climbing up a pyramid. You can get to the top of the pyramid and be a highly conscious or mindful person. You will be liberated upon exiting from the top of the pyramid.

CHAPTER 11

The Purpose of Self-Reflections

Self-reflection is the process of checking on our thoughts, emotions, communication, and actions or behavior. The purpose of self-reflection is to ensure that we are deeply aware of ourselves so that we do not let our intrapersonal issues affect our sense of functioning, and the well-being of others. Self-reflections help to nurture our personal and spiritual growth.

Be wary of unresolved issues. Unresolved issues are past bad experiences and unhealthy conditioning that we went through in our life journey. These issues lead us to an unhealed (wounded) stage.

Know your life lessons. It is wonderful to learn lessons from past bad experiences and conditioning. But we should be alert and aware so that these experiences do not cloud our thoughts, emotions, communication, and actions. Past experiences should guide and help us to overcome life challenges and not hinder our growth.

WHY DO PAINS AND SUFFERING REMAIN?

During self-reflection, it is crucial to be brutally honest with ourselves. When self-reflection isn't done honestly, people continuously go through pains and suffering. They will drown themselves in misery and cause misery to others. Poor self-reflective skills imprison us in a state of metaphysical sleep.

I have come across many who write journals and do self-reflections but remain trapped in deep suffering and lack clarity on what to do to make their lives better. In the past, I used to reflect on my negative behavior but continued behaving the same way after reflection. After exploring deeper, I realized that *brutal honesty* during reflections and *conscious actions* after reflections were missing, and so I continued with my negative behavior. If we lack self-honesty, then we are bound to the forms of reasoning that arise from the ego.

The ego is a metaphysical sleeping pill
that keeps a person in a metaphysical sleep.

CHAPTER 12

GRADES OF SELF-REFLECTIONS

TO PROGRESS FROM THE FIRST level of reflection to the highest grade, I created three grades of self-reflections for an easier understanding and application: biases, morals, and wisdom. I conceptualized these three types of reflections as a way to relieve oneself of pain and suffering and to merge with the supreme truth of the existence. It worked for me, and I trust that it will be of immense help to you.

The first grade of reflection is what I call viewpoint reasoning and rationalizing. In this method of self-reflection, a person makes sense of situations, thoughts, emotions, communication, or actions by matching them to their narratives. These narratives are their own beliefs, perceptions, and biases, which they consider to be the truth. An example would be, "I stole money because I need to feed my family. There is nothing wrong in my actions because I do not hold a stable job." Reflections are done by matching narratives to justify their actions. These narratives are usually stereotypes, judgmental and distorted perspectives that arise due to biases and ego.

The second grade of reflection is also viewpoint reasoning and rationalizing, but based on an individual's moral principles. For example, "No matter how many financial challenges I face, I will not borrow money from my friends. Borrowing money is not part of my values, and I believe it is not a good habit." Reflections are done by matching them with moral principles.

The third grade is the highest form of reflection, as these reflections are done with wisdom. It is about matching your reflections with the responses and answers of existence. This type of reflection has no rigidity and works beyond theoretical knowledge. I call these intuitive reflections. These reflections create a balance between logical and intuitive reasoning skills.

When doing intuitive reflection, one has to tune the mind, heart, and body in symphony. In this type of reflection, one has to be very highly aware. The first step is that we have to be fully aware of how our ego functions. The second step is to be aware of how our metaphysical sleep conditions connect to our ego (see chapter 8) and cloud our intuitive reflections. The third step is to completely distance yourself from the ego and then start your reflections.

The last step is to match the answers you get from your reflections with existence's responses through a strong sense of intuition. This intuition is the bridge between you and your existence. To raise intuition and receive clear answers from intuition, one has to be meditative.

The mind holds our intellect (borrowed knowledge), and the heart holds intuition. A clear answer reaches us only when the mind, heart, and body are in harmony. When reflecting from the mind alone, a person reflects as an intellectual person. Reflecting on the body alone makes one an instinctual person. But when the mind, heart, and body are in harmony, there is reflection as an intelligent person. This reflection is empirical. One would be able to fathom these types of intuitive reflections only through spiritual experiences.

FIVE STEPS TO THE HIGHEST GRADE OF REFLECTIONS

1. Meditate first.
2. Keep a distance from your ego and any metaphysical sleep conditions that connect to your ego before doing reflections. This distance strengthens your self-honesty so that reflection will give you clear answers.
3. Connect these clear answers with your intuition to sharpen your clarity.
4. The final results will amaze you and bring you to the highest wisdom.
5. Practice, practice, and practice. These types of reflections need spiritual experiences and practice.

I learned that there are two vital keys to attaining the highest qualitative state of self-reflection. First, be brutally honest *to* yourself *about* yourself, and second, practice meditation daily.

To do authentic self-reflection, open the heart's windows and allow the breeze of intuition to flow in.

CHAPTER 13

ELEVEN TOOLS FOR GOOD SELF-REFLECTIONS

THERE ARE THE ELEVEN GUIDING tools that I apply in my life to ensure that I remain on the right track when it comes to self-reflection. I believe these will be helpful for you too.

1. Practice honesty when going deeper into understanding your issues. The more honest you are, the easier it is to see and accept the truth and change for the better.
2. Stop overly externalizing blame. Take personal responsibility.
3. Be very watchful over your ego-hindering reflections.
4. Check on the viewpoint from which you use reasoning and rationalizing methods in your reflections so as not to gratify your ego.
5. Are you reflecting based on biases (first grade), morals (second grade), or wisdom (highest grade)?
6. Keep a distance between your thoughts, emotions, and yourself when doing reflections. This method enhances clarity.

7. Never get entangled with the noise in the mind when reflecting. Reflection is not a noisy transaction. Remember that we will face difficulties finding the needle in a haystack; therefore, never reflect with a clouded mind and emotions.
8. Never reflect when you are mentally, emotionally, and physically exhausted and affected.
9. Never do reflections under the influence of substances like alcohol.
10. Never reflect when you are thrilled and excited. Always try to stay calm and grounded when reflecting; it helps you to receive clear and conscious answers.
11. The best reflections are achieved after meditation; it raises clarity after the mind is calm and grounded.

Self-reflections are moments of clairvoyance and solace you reap from existence. Write your life journals together with existence, and you will hit the bull's eye.

CHAPTER 14

MEDITATION IS A COSMIC ROMANCE

WE MIGHT HAVE HEARD AND come across this word "meditation" many times in our lives. When we are flooded with pains and suffering, a therapist or a spiritual guru would tell us to "meditate." Sometimes we are advised to breathe in and out consciously to calm ourselves before carrying out any important task. This approach helps to reduce tension and anxiety.

The more consciously these inhalations and exhalations are done, the better we feel and think. This process of inhalation and exhalation of breath is a meditation method.

Many questions may arise in our minds about what meditation does. What happens during and after meditation? What are some of our assumptions about meditation? I hope this book will guide you logically and intuitively to find these answers. The answers may not awaken one immediately from metaphysical sleep, as awakening is a gradual process for which daily time and effort are needed. The answers you find in this book will supplement and facilitate your spiritual journey towards cosmic consciousness—the state of self-realization where we realize our oneness with existence.

So what is meditation? Meditation is attaining the state of thoughtlessness and then transcending into the super and cosmic consciousness. The ultimate purpose of meditation is to still our minds and bring us into the present moment. When we are in the present moment, our mind stops wandering into the past and future. With consistent practice of keeping our minds in the present moment, we will gradually transcend into the state of thoughtlessness, superconsciousness, and cosmic consciousness.

Meditation creates a distance between yourself, the mind and body. This distance holds a space, and that space is the space of consciousness where thoughts cease. Meditation methods (working on stilling the mind) are processes, and meditation (the mind is stilled) is the outcome.

I have experience doing various methods of meditation, and I would say all of them work effectively. However, some meditation methods are easy, and some are challenging. Among the various meditation methods I tried, I would say the most challenging are the mantra meditations. In mantra meditation, you have to chant a spiritual syllable. Each syllable holds a strong vibration that connects to universal powers for protection, guidance, and liberation. The spiritual verse holds specific energies that dissolve negativity and bestows positivity on the individual. These mantra meditations even have the power to make us sweat in an air-conditioned room. Mantra meditations are like intense astral-cardio workouts that provide immense benefits and results to a person.

I would say that meditation is a cosmic romance. Through meditation, we build deep intimate connections with existence (the universe, the higher or divine powers). The spiritual powers that existence holds are omnipotent, omnipresent, and omniscient. Through meditation, we are liberated from pain and suffering and transcend into the state of blissfulness as we get blessed with these spiritual powers of existence.

Meditation connects us to our higher selves by aligning the mind, physical body, and subtle bodies with the cosmic energies of existence. Through consistent practice of meditation, we can gradually merge with the divine and end our suffering and pain. Meditation is also an act of centering and balancing of masculine and feminine energies within a person. During meditation as the masculine and feminine energies in a person merge together, this leads to enlightenment.

Esoterically, meditation is the inward sexual union of feminine and masculine energies.

CHAPTER 15

Why We Need Meditation?

I WAS ABLE TO WEED OUT parts of unconsciousness and plant seeds of higher consciousness within myself through meditations. I was able to use my bitter life experiences as lessons to grow my consciousness. I learned to transform negative moments into moments of spiritual growth. All this happened through my daily practice of meditation.

Meditation releases us from the pains and suffering of life. It helps us to understand ourselves and our birth purpose.

About Suffering and Pains

There are two types of suffering: interpersonal and intrapersonal. Our transactions with other people and situations cause *interpersonal* suffering. Imagine meeting someone who keeps criticizing and demoralizing you, so that you tend to suffer in their presence. These are external factors. Interpersonal suffering arises through relating with people and environment.

An environment becomes exhausting if the place is packed with challenging people and situations.

The other type of suffering is *intrapersonal*, which means it happens within us—we are responsible for our inner "heaven and hell." Our own thoughts and emotions torment us. These are internal factors. Intrapersonal suffering arises from our way of relating to ourselves.

These two types of suffering give us lots of pain. The pains can be mental, emotional, or psychosomatic symptoms. The mind and the body are connected systems; one part affects the other. Mental and emotional pains can give pain to the physical parts of the body. Physical pains are also signals that explain blockages in our mental, emotional, and energy fields.

So, the next time you are going through suffering and pain, it is good to look inwards (at yourself) and outwards (at the people, situations, and environments around you). Be wary of externalizing all problems. We should always work on checking and correcting our unconscious issues as well. A tremendous amount of self-healing is imperative when it comes to ending our suffering and pains. To self-heal, we first need to develop a profound understanding of ourselves.

The Clouded Mind and Emotions

A clouded mind holds biases, distorted perceptions, limiting beliefs, perplexity, and all kinds of pain-causing thoughts that are either ours or borrowed from others. Clouded emotions are ungrounded emotions of anger, envy, jealousy, hatred, anxiety, sadness, and other pressing emotions. We have to be aware that these clouded thoughts and emotions are tied to our ego and affect our clear perceptions.

I am not saying ego is entirely wrong. Clear thoughts and grounded emotions bring out a healthy ego. An example of a healthy ego is self-respect, possessing good values, and being a disciplined person. This type of healthy ego delivers constructive outcomes. An unhealthy ego is destructive. An unhealthy ego causes a person to act negatively. If the ego is not managed well, it can take a harmful direction.

Here is an example. My healthy ego teaches me to apply positive values in my life situations. When the ego functions with unawareness, I start to force and impose my values onto others and suffocate others by making them believe my way is the right or the best way. The ego is a double-edged sword with constructive and destructive attributes. It takes wisdom and intuition to experience and comprehend the truths and workings of the ego.

HOW DOES MEDITATION HELP?

Meditation raises our sense of clarity in knowing about ourselves and builds our ability to study people and situations with clear perceptions. I will define clarity as to the ability to see through things without clouded thoughts and emotions. Meditation works by cleaning up thoughts and emotions that do not serve a positive purpose in our lives. Meditation creates a distance between us and our thoughts and brings us into a space of consciousness. As we move towards this space, we gradually dissolve our pains and suffering. With consistent practice of meditation, we will raise our consciousness, and develop the ability to evaluate without ego-driven judgments.

Meditation metamorphoses darkness
and emanates light within and around you.

CHAPTER 16

What Are Enlightenment and Liberation?

SATORI ARE MINI ENLIGHTENING MOMENTS. I have experienced satori and am sharing these with you so that we can walk together towards liberation.

Spiritual enlightenment and liberation will mean reaching a state of self-realization—transcending the physical state of material identification to attain the subtle state of superconsciousness and cosmic consciousness.

The *physical* state is the state whereby we are identified with our mind and body. When I say "I," I refer to the state of my body and my mind. This dimension describes physical identification, a duality where you and the existence are perceived as two separate entities. For example, I am a human being, and I live in this existence.

The *cosmic* state is transcending into self-realization. It is also the state of non-duality, the realization that we are one with existence. The existence and I are not separate entities, and we are one. The cosmic state is metaphysically described as our inner light merging with the divine light or our truth merging with the supreme truth.

Liberation means gaining freedom from pain and suffering and attaining a state of bliss.

These processes begin once we start doing our daily meditations and practice being conscious of our daily actions.

I have kept this chapter on enlightenment and liberation short as enlightenment and liberation are states that must be experienced, in order to understand deeply about the euphoric and blissful rewards of existence. To experience these states, consistent meditative practices must be performed. This book is designed to help you progress on the path to enlightenment and liberation.

Meditations and conscious actions align our energies with cosmic energies. These cosmic energies illuminate our inner light and open doors for liberation.

CHAPTER 17

QUESTIONS AND ANSWERS ABOUT PEOPLE WHO MEDITATE

MANY PEOPLE HAVE ASKED ME questions about meditations, and I have chosen to answer them in this book to share with readers. These answers come from life experiences and knowledge gained from mystic teachers.

1. **Does a meditative person get angry?**

   Yes, some meditating people have a heightened sense of sensitivity. They could see through conscious and unconscious thoughts, emotions, communication, and actions of themselves and others. They usually get angry over people's unconscious behaviors that cause pain and suffering to themselves and others. This type of anger is a righteous one. Righteous anger is anger that is aligned with the cosmic energies of existence. A meditative person also gradually develops an ability to express his anger in a grounded manner.

2. **Does meditation cause you to lose sexual energy?**

Meditation raises the sexual energy inwardly, and the meditator develops the ability to transform these energies into constructive forms. Sexual energy is transformed, not lost.

3. **Does meditation make a person respectful towards people who are older or higher in social status?**

A meditative person respects all lives equally. A meditator holds reverence for existence. Respect is a quality earned from a person's way of relating to other living beings.

4. **Do meditative people have bad habits?**

Meditative people may have bad habits. However, they either let go of them or learn to work with them consciously. Meditation does overcome compulsive and addictive behaviors.

5. **Do meditative people have desires?**

They do have desires, but they learn how to control desires and not get consumed by them. They let go of desires that don't serve constructive purposes or cause pains and suffering. As they progress to higher states of consciousness, they gradually free themselves from all kinds of desires.

6. **Do meditators hold strong bonds?**

They love unconditionally without self-interest or a possessive nature. However, they remain emotionally detached from worldly and illusionary bondages. Therefore, their strong bonds are connected to only existence.

7. **Why doesn't meditation work for some people?**

Meditation must be done correctly and consistently to work.

8. **How do you know if the method of meditation is incorrect?**

During incorrect meditations, the mind wanders in the past and future. The meditator is entangled in the illusionary pain and pleasures of the mind. And usually, the meditator doesn't practice awareness in bringing the mind back into the present moment.

9. **Is it natural for the mind to wander?**

Yes, it is natural for the mind to wander, but the meditator should try to bring the mind into a meditative state. The existence is not going to punish the meditator for allowing the mind to wander. The existence appreciates and blesses if the meditator takes efforts to still the wandering mind. Gentle efforts to come back to the present state without fighting and struggling with thoughts are needed during meditation.

10. **How does one remain in a meditative state?**

Imagine watching a movie. We can watch the movie, but we do not enter into the movie and become one of the actors in the movie. In the same way, we practice awareness by watching our wandering thoughts but remaining unaffected and detached from the thoughts. We do not become the thought.

Meditation becomes shaky when the meditator gets hooked and entangled to thoughts and remains in this entangled process throughout the meditation. In other words, meditation shouldn't become what has been called a closed-eye daydreaming process.

If you are entangled in thoughts at any point in time, become aware and return to the present state. Do not follow your thoughts—only watch them at a distance during meditation.

To know about how and why meditators function in a certain way
is to meditate. The best way to unravel mysticism
is to experience it.

CHAPTER 18

SEEDS OF CONSCIOUSNESS

TO GROW OUR CONSCIOUSNESS, WE need to work on cultivating good qualities. To grow well, a plant needs seeds, water, good soil, sunlight, and nutrients. Likewise, qualities of higher consciousness also get seeded in us as we raise our sense of consciousness.

In chapter 29, "Energy Consciousness," I will briefly discuss about chakras. As our energy rises through these chakras, we develop qualities of higher consciousness. These qualities facilitate the growth of our consciousness. It is good to start practicing these qualities while simultaneously working on growing our consciousness through meditation.

"Weeding" is removing parts of unconsciousness, and "seeding" is planting qualities of higher consciousness. For the next eight chapters, I will take you through the seeds of consciousness. Each chapter is written from my spiritual experiences and the lessons I learned from self-realized mystic teachers.

Of course, there are many seeds of higher consciousness, but I will share eight of the most vital ones:

1. compassion
2. faith
3. forgiveness
4. letting go
5. gratitude
6. love
7. acceptance and trust
8. sensitivity

As part of daily spiritual practice,
eliminate the demon of unconsciousness
and initiate the angels of consciousness in yourself.

CHAPTER 19

COMPASSION

BEING COMPASSIONATE IS A GREAT way to remain calm and practice a nonaggressive approach towards the unconscious actions of others. As we become more and more meditative, we can see the unconsciousness in us and others. As we practice being more conscious, we will experience righteous anger or some natural form of irritancy when we encounter the unconscious actions of others. It is good to practice compassion when we encounter such situations. I used these methods to strengthen my power of compassion when I encounter difficult situations with unconscious people.

Practice empathy. When you look at the behavior of unconscious people, have empathy towards them. Speak to them about how their unconscious behavior is causing problems for them and others. Apply empathy when they anger you and make you frustrated. Practice empathy and explain your points clearly to help an unconscious person awaken from their metaphysical sleep.

Practice letting it be. Let it be if an unconscious person does not understand your points and doesn't agree with your statements; you did your part to explain. You have actually planted a seed in their garden of unconsciousness. Hence, you may leave the situation as it is and move on. Do keep in mind that too much exhausting efforts on your part to fight your points will slowly drag you into their pit of unconsciousness. While practicing compassion for others, practice self-compassion for yourself as well.

Watch your ego. Never let ego take control of the situation. Do not react, but respond with compassion.

What if I couldn't practice compassion due to my anger when dealing with the unconscious actions of people?

Practice grounded aggression. Sometimes it is difficult to control your temper for a long time, especially if the unconscious behavior of the other party is getting out of control. Keep in mind that anger cannot be controlled, suppressed, or repressed for a long time. Anger is a form of energy that can be transformed and should not be swept under the carpet. If someone asks you to control, suppress, or repress any thought or emotion, they teach you to be unconscious.

In such cases, practice grounded aggression. Grounded aggression means using your anger and not losing it. It means constructively transforming your anger. For example, to deal with difficult communications, you may state your points firmly, clearly, and consciously. Instead of raising your voice, you could raise your words. You can ask clarifying questions and give feedback that you intuit might awaken the unconscious and argumentative person.

CHAPTER 20

FAITH

WHEN WE TALK ABOUT FAITH, we are talking about holding onto trust attached to a higher power—the existence. This trust is like a bridge between you and the universe. Faith is having trust in your heart that the existence will always help you. This faith happens when the mind and heart are in harmony.

Let me share an example of how faith works. When my thoughts tell me that I will not score well on my exams, I still have a solid inner feeling in me that says, "You may not score well, but you will never fail the exams, as the existence will protect you from failures."

We should create harmony between the mind and the heart. If we are deeply connected to the mind, we will not comprehend the messages conveyed deep in the heart. When I say "heart," I am not referring to emotions. *Heart* means intuition, and *mind* means intellect. Emotions are feelings that are generated from the intellect. Relying solely on the mind's answers will not help us in strengthening faith. Depending too much on the mind simply raises fear, doubt, perplexity, and unconscious actions. Keep in mind that a rational person and an emotional person are both obedient to the mind's orders. Being entirely a slave to the mind does affect our sense of faith. Mind raises doubt and fear, and doubt and fear slowly pollute faith. Therefore, one should practice mastering the mind when it comes to developing solid faith.

To have a clear sense of faith, the mind and the heart should work in harmony. With faith, we can achieve positivity and success in our actions. A daily gratitude prayer and meditation will help this process.

I learned that we need to put in our efforts and practice qualities of higher consciousness for spiritual growth. Existence reciprocates to our efforts. Without efforts, faith, and other sublime qualities of higher consciousness, we will face challenges in procuring the best results for spiritual growth.

CHAPTER 21

FORGIVENESS

Forgiveness is a practice applied to relieve oneself from pain and suffering. It works well as part of a self-healing process. There are two types of forgiveness: one is about forgiving ourselves, and the other is about forgiving others. Both types work towards improving the mental and emotional well-being of the forgiver. These methods of forgiving are to cleanse our minds from negative thoughts that hinder our spiritual progression.

Forgiving Others

Forgiving others may heal us, but existence still makes the final decision on granting forgiveness. Although forgiveness is therapeutic for us, we should still understand it from a spiritual dimension. We should be aware that we do not hold the right to forgive anyone. We came to the universe to serve the price of our unconscious actions, battling our pains and suffering. We can say to a person, "I forgive you," and a month later the person may still suffer consequences for his past malicious actions against us. Therefore, we should always be clear that existence makes the final decisions regarding granting forgiveness.

SELF-FORGIVENESS

The best way to practice forgiveness is to ask for forgiveness from the existence for yourself, and then to forgive yourself. Speak to the existence directly and ask forgiveness for yourself. Asking forgiveness for yourself is a prayerful communication between you and the existence.

The existence does help us to heal. We can work on our self-forgiveness, but we have to keep in mind that the existence will not forgive others immediately after we have forgiven them. The existence has its own set of laws when it comes to granting forgiveness. To benefit your healing process, you may forgive in your heart the person who has caused you harm, but never expect the existence to grant your wishes for forgiveness for others immediately.

I always seek self-forgiveness and ask for the existence's inner guidance to help me awaken from my unconscious actions. Most of the time, my request for forgiveness is for my unconscious actions. This method is similar to self-forgiveness. For example, as I apologize to the existence, I simultaneously tell myself to forgive my errors. Practicing these forgiving methods helps me to relieve from negative thoughts and emotions.

CHAPTER 22

LETTING GO

LETTING GO MEANS RELEASING MATTERS that affect your personal and spiritual growth. Here are five ways to let go that I use. These five methods helped me in my spiritual journey.

1. Let go of habits that jeopardize your consciousness; for example, smoking, drinking, drugs, or pornography.
2. Let go of peers who exhaust your internal energy; for example, people who demoralize you.
3. Let go of an environment that hinders your personal and spiritual growth; for example, a troubled workplace.
4. Let go of thoughts, emotions, communication, and actions that do not serve any positive outcome for you. For example, do not waste time on small talk, gossip, and finding fault in others; instead, use that time to do physical workouts or meditations.
5. Letting go also means "let it be." For example, if you cannot do anything about a situation, or it doesn't cause any negative impact on your consciousness, then you might just let it be. Never listen to your ego and try to provoke, resist, or fight redundant and unnecessary

> situations. An example of a redundant action would be showing too much curiosity about the personal lives of others, and then comparing your life with theirs to seek validation for yourself or make yourself "feel better."

Letting go is not about avoiding life's challenges. The challenges of life teach us many lessons. The existence assigns challenges to use to help us grow. We should face our challenges with courage and work through them, growing in this way our experience, intelligence, and consciousness.

The existence works in a way that makes life happen for us and not against us. Thus, it is essential to be wary of what we let go. If we let go of challenges, we are letting go of golden opportunities that enhance the growth of our consciousness.

CHAPTER 23

GRATITUDE

GRATITUDE IS THE MOST VITAL seed of spiritual growth. Practicing gratitude is simple. It is saying thank you to existence for all the good things that are granted to us. Here I will share five great benefits of gratitude that my spiritual teachers and I reaped.

1. Learn to appreciate the goodness in our lives. Gratitude helps us to eliminate negative thoughts and emotions.
2. The existence responds with an abundance of positivity when we express gratitude.
3. With gratitude, we will remain contented, happy, and healthy.
4. Gratitude helps us in mental, emotional, physical, and spiritual self-healing.
5. Gratitude grows our qualities of consciousness.

What is the opposite of gratitude? Complaining and unappreciation. To lack gratitude is to complain about life and not appreciate the good things that happen in life. These are adverse reactions and not positive responses. The existence reacts to complaints and comparisons by returning us more pain and suffering. We reap what we sow, and the existence reciprocates to what we give it.

TWO WAYS TO PRACTICE GRATITUDE

1. Use a notebook or journal to write down the things that make you feel thankful.
2. Talk directly to the existence after meditation, and thank existence for the good things in our lives. For example, you can read from your notebook, either aloud or silently. Speaking directly to the existence to express my gratitude is one of my favorite ways. I have expressed gratitude in silence and through a clear, audible tone. Both ways, I experienced existence responding to me with positivity.

CHAPTER 24

LOVE

LOVE IS A DEEP CONNECTION between you and the universe. The sexual energy inside a person transformed into energies of worship, service, and exuberance becomes love energy. Love is a form of energy that doesn't obey and abide by the demanding logic of the mind. Love is a quality of higher consciousness; it is from the heart chakra, as we will learn in the chapters about chakras.

After meditations, I always use these three beautiful phrases to build a strong intimate relationship with existence: "I am sorry, I thank you, and I love you, existence." Self-forgiveness, gratitude, and love are the sweet spots of communicating with existence.

UNDERSTANDING LOVE

When the mind prepares conditions for love to happen, it is not love. Love is not bound to the conditions of the mind. To understand love, one has to experience it. We humans have defined love in many ways, but when defined by existence, love is seen as unconditional, ever-relating, and ever-flowing like a river. It is simply an act of positive giving without expecting anything in return.

LOVE AND THE EXISTENCE

When we love ourselves, humanity, and existence, we engage in activities that contribute positively to existence. We avoid harmful activities that don't benefit existence. Love helps us to see every living thing in this world as part of us. Love helps us to realize that existence and all living beings are parts of our consciousness.

Likewise, when you truly love a person, you do not break their inner peace, boundaries, and happiness. You do not force them to meet your needs and expectations. When you are in love, you are in a flow of constant relating. You do not disturb or destroy something you love. You simply water it and enjoy watching it grow beautifully—in the same way we water our consciousness and watch it grow towards self-realization and oneness with existence.

The pathway to higher consciousness is the love for existence, the love for the lives of existence, and the love for oneself. Meditation, the cosmic romance with existence, is a form of deep love for knowing and realizing the supreme truth. This love is unconditional, ever-relating, and everlasting.

CHAPTER 25

ACCEPTANCE AND TRUST

ACCEPTANCE IS TAKING A NON-RESISTIVE approach when communicating with the existence. Acceptance is a quality that is supported by love and trust between us and existence. If we love and trust existence deeply, we know that existence brings in only situations that contribute to our spiritual development.

I learned that it is imperative to have a clean and harmless heart, which means not causing harm to yourself and any living beings in existence. Through daily meditations and practicing the qualities of higher consciousness, I have come to understand that existence brings into my life only situations that benefit my consciousness.

Acceptance helps us be aware that there are no problems—problems are just illusions of the mind, and we have to accept and work through a situation. If the situations are painful, we can do two things: face it and overcome it, or let it pass if our methods of dealing with the situations didn't work. Both ways of handling the situations render lessons that are useful for the growth of our consciousness.

Sometimes a challenge enters our lives to relay a message and provide a lesson, and it is not always about finding solutions.

Acceptance and trust help us see through a situation and give us the wisdom to take suitable actions.

You will face more formidable challenges when dealing with situations if your options are beyond your control. For example, it would be enervating to you to completely change the behavior of an unconscious troublemaker. However, you can work on explaining your points clearly and consciously. If things don't work out well, let go of your exhausting communications and leave the situation. A prolonged difficult communication with an unconscious troublemaker might drag you into his world of unconsciousness.

As you deal with difficult situations, you need to be alert in intuitively listening to the existence's messages within you. That's where qualities of love, trust, and acceptance come in. Resistance and struggles will drag you into the web of unconsciousness and raise your pain and suffering. On the other hand, acceptance of a situation and trust in existence makes you handle situations consciously and intelligently.

When I encounter difficult situations, I accept that I am facing challenges for the growth of my consciousness. Acceptance helps me merge with the challenging situation courageously. I don't avoid challenges, and I work on remaining fully present in the flow. I place my trust in the existence to help walk me through challenges with its guidance, and doing so has helped me to understand that there are no real problems but only situations for growth. These practices of acceptance work well through regular meditations. It may be hard to accept challenges initially, but with the gradual practice of this quality and regular meditation, acceptance becomes easy.

CHAPTER 26

SENSITIVITY

SENSITIVITY IS A BEAUTIFUL QUALITY that grows in us innately as we raise our consciousness. How does sensitivity help us in raising our consciousness? Let me explain some ways how it works.

In today's world, a sensitive person may be seen as someone who gets hurt or angry quickly. Some people call themselves "sensitive," but they go around hurting others and work hard to protect themselves. That's not how sensitivity works, from a spiritual dimension. Sensitivity is an act of selflessness.

Sensitivity is the heightened ability to sense. If we are sensitive to our thoughts and emotions, we will be very sharp and alert about how these thoughts and emotions affect us. A sensitive person is a very aware person. Being aware helps one raise consciousness. Therefore, sensitivity is an excellent quality of consciousness.

A sensitive person knows about pain very well. Hence, a sensitive person works consciously to prevent causing harm to the self and to other living things in existence. A sensitive person is conscious of communication and actions towards others. A harmless nature is a quality of sensitivity. Feeling sensitive over the pain of others is a healer's quality. With sensitivity, one can work delicately to heal the pains and suffering of themselves and others.

As sensitivity grows awareness and alertness, sensitive people are generally alert and can detach themselves from the painful actions of unconsciousness. A sensitive person can remain unentangled with the bondages of pains and suffering. For example, while everyone knows that boiling water produces a lot of heat, a sensitive person can feel and experience the heat more strongly and will be more careful and conscious in ensuring the hot water is handled safely and put to proper use.

A sensitive person remains sharp and alert to subtle messages from existence. Sensitivity helps one to connect and communicate easily with existence. A sensitive person can see, hear, feel, and read spiritual signs everywhere in existence. Extrasensory perception is a quality that arises from a heightened sense of sensitivity too. Mind, emotions, body, and energy will be brought to greater heights if one practices sensitivity in daily life affairs.

Meditation has helped me to raise my level of sensitivity. I became more mindful or conscious of my thoughts, emotions, communication, and actions. Sensitivity grew my qualities of empathy, compassion, and love. I became able to understand my pain and the pain of others.

CHAPTER 27

Consciousness of the Mind and Emotions

The mind, emotions, physique (body) and spirit (energy) are like four rooms. They play a crucial role in supporting spiritual development. To rise into higher realms of consciousness, a person should make conscious efforts in caring for these four rooms. Let me guide you on understanding and caring for these four rooms. I will talk about the mind and emotions in this chapter and about the body and energy in chapters 28 and 29.

The Dark Shadows

Dark shadows are parts of our unconsciousness. When I say "dark shadows," I am referring to one's negative thoughts and emotions. Negative thoughts and emotions cause unconscious communication and actions. The mind is a pool of thoughts and generates emotions. Painful thoughts create painful emotions, and happy thoughts create happy emotions.

There are three ways to managing and caring for our thoughts and emotions. One is to meditate, the second is to reflect, and the last is to acknowledge our dark shadows and remain conscious about not feeding and supplementing them. Self-control plays a crucial role in not feeding and supplementing our dark shadows.

Feeding your dark side means indulging in activities that exacerbate your suffering. For example, watching pornography, smoking, drinking, or taking drugs may appear to be temporary coping methods to calm down urges and pain, but these activities are a gateway to addiction. We are feeding our dark shadows and making them grow more potent with bad habits. We are diving deeper into the well of unconsciousness.

We supplement our dark shadows by associating with materials that cause us pains and suffering. For example, if you have stopped consuming alcohol, but you still mix with peers who are heavy drinkers, then there is a possibility that you might relapse.

So what can we do? We can stop doing what blunts our consciousness and hinders our progress towards raising consciousness. To know how to stop, we need to study ourselves, check on our unconscious parts, and start taking actions to prevent further inner destruction. That also means staying away from people, conversations, and environments that affect our minds and emotions. If we choose to make clean decisions, we should make them firmly and never indulge in any activities that cause further harm to our mental and emotional well-being.

I know it may be challenging to work through. But efforts are needed to see results when it comes to connecting with existence and raising our consciousness.

Practice Self-Control

Practicing self-control is challenging if one is trapped in addiction. To overcome addictive cycles, I would say that it is good to go through therapeutic interventions. However, here are some simple steps I practiced that worked for me. You can give these methods a try to see if they work for you too.

Step 1: Awareness

The first step to practicing self-control is to look at the desire, craving, or need visiting your mind and become completely aware of it. Never try to resist it or fight it. Each time you resist or fight it, you suppress it. When an unconscious part of you or a dark shadow gets suppressed, it will multiply and come back stronger. And when you resist it or fight it, you will visualize it all the more. For example, I tell you to stop thinking about an elephant, and guess what? The next moment, your mind starts showing you images of elephants. Therefore, instead of fighting and resisting, be aware. But when I say "be aware," I also mean keeping a distance between yourself and the pressing thoughts.

Be aware of two types of ignorance when practicing self-control. First, we may be unaware of our unconscious parts and release them onto others carelessly. Second, we may be aware of our dark shadows or unconscious parts but we are not taking any actions to work on them. These two types of ignorance destroy our peace and the peace of others.

To practice self-control, self-awareness has to be raised. Self-awareness is not just about knowing about the light and darkness in yourself; it is also the ability to use your light and darkness for the growth of your consciousness and not allowing your darkness to harm yourself and others.

STEP 2: ACCESSIBILITY

The second step is to cut down and limit exposure to any persons, communications, activities, and environments that lead to losing self-control or affect mental and emotional health. For example, if you are working on quitting smoking, it is good to cut down the cigarettes, limit hanging around peers who indulge in such habits, and stay away from environments that encourage you to light a cigarette. However, you do not have to stick to these routines your entire life; as long as you are confident that external stressors no longer affect your internal energy, you may start returning to regular routines. But when you are just starting to practice your self-control methods, it is good to apply these steps.

The best way to work with limiting and cutting down exposure is by asking yourself whether these persons, communications, activities, and environments are harmful to your mental, emotional, physical, and spiritual well-being. If they are harmful, then control your access to them and their accessibility to you.

Don't use any maladaptive methods such as regret, guilt, suppression, repression, biased reasoning, or tiring ways to deal with these challenging moments. Maladaptive coping methods may help you cope for a short period, but they would aggravate your pains in the long run. In some situations, these maladaptive methods could cause your thoughts and emotions to exist passively.

STEP 3: CONTENTMENT

Contentment requires practice. Be content with what you have in this moment. How? Practice gratitude exercises. When we express gratitude for what we have, we naturally make our minds contented and happy. A contented mind remains still and undisturbed. It doesn't fight or follow thoughts of pain and temptations. There is nothing wrong with having desires—desires motivate us to achieve what we need. However, a mind that houses too many desires may not be able to live in peace. A person first develops a desire, but then desire controls him, leading to pains and suffering and dragging a person into lower levels of consciousness.

POINTS TO NOTE

- If you take care of your thoughts, your emotions will be well-managed.
- Resisting, struggling, fighting, lamenting, suppressing, or repressing forcefully only multiplies tempting and painful thoughts.
- Self-control is the key that opens the doors to balancing thoughts and emotions. Self-control is a promising practice that leads you to higher consciousness without any self-imposed pressure.
- Painful thoughts and emotions are surmountable with self-control and the daily practice of meditation.
- To practice self-control, raise self-awareness, recognize the limits of accessibility, and practice self-contentment.
- Meditate daily and practice qualities of higher consciousness.
- Meditation will guide you through more profound ways of strengthening your mental and emotional energies, and will help you close the mental and emotional doors that beckon harmful activities.

Professionally, I work with the mental and emotional needs of people. Mind and emotions form cause-and-effect chains for understanding suffering and pain. Humans are born with mental health challenges that also severely affect their emotional states. I am writing this book to reach out to those who are still able to comprehend my message and can manage their thoughts and emotions to a reasonably good extent.

If anyone is going through severe challenges in managing their thoughts and emotions, then I would say it is good to consult proper help from medical professionals. Never impose this knowledge on someone who is experiencing severe mental health challenges. Our existence has created us so that each of our paths is different. Therefore, it is always good to respect everyone's path and to allow everyone to flourish within their capability.

Knowing there are transcendental conditions for every person in spiritual development, it is always good to plant seeds of awakening without imposing values. Wisdom allows every person to shine at their zenith spiritually.

CHAPTER 28

Body Consciousness

THE BODY IS LIKE A temple that houses our consciousness. A healthy body is needed to raise our consciousness. If we suffer from bodily aches and diseases, our bodies feel pain. Pain is the body's way of telling us that something isn't right, and it is our responsibility to attend to the pain and cure it.

Think of the body as the bridge between us and existence. If the bridge is unstable and wobbly, it'll be difficult for us to cross it to connect with existence. We will face fear every time as to whether the bridge might break and cause us to fall. In the same way, if we invest a vast amount of our time to repair the problems in our bodies, we will spend less time thinking about connecting with the existence.

We should always remember that an unhealthy body and mind aren't supportive peers when raising our consciousness. When pain enters our mind and body, it is our responsibility to alleviate it. If we aren't taking the proper remedies, this pain resides in us and becomes an obstacle to our spiritual progression.

The mind and the body are connected. What happens in the mind affects the body, and what happens in the body affects the mind. For example, when you have many painful thoughts in your mind and are constantly disturbed by these thoughts, you will later develop a headache.

I find these three ways helpful in caring for our body and preparing it for spiritual development: hygiene, exercise, and food.

HYGIENE

The body has to be kept clean. The body's cleanliness indirectly affects the mind and emotions. Every day, we regularly meet up with different people and hang around in different environments. Our body absorbs different types of dust and energies. Energies that we absorb affect the way we function (think, feel, communicate, and act). We will talk about energies more deeply in the next chapter.

Sometimes, cleaning our rooms makes us feel happy and energetic, or we feel joyful after a shower. These types of cleaning and cleansing are forms of recharging our bodies and energies. Having a good sense of personal hygiene helps us remove unwanted energies that might hinder our progress towards consciousness. Keeping the body clean is imperative when working towards spiritual progression. An unhygienic body hosts illness and diseases, which in turn affect spiritual progression. When we meditate after a shower, it is like cleaning up our prayer rooms before doing prayers. By showing respect and love to our body, we also show our love, respect, and gratitude to existence.

EXERCISE

The body needs exercise to keep it healthy and to achieve spiritual goals. Spiritual fitness is about doing exercises that increase the body's flexibility, reduce pains and aches, increase healing, and raise energy levels and bodily strengths.

Spiritual fitness is about having a body that remains healthy and energetic, which supports spiritual progression. A healthy and energetic body can sit long for meditations without distractions.

We need to sit in an upright position, keeping our spines straight, when doing meditations. Body aches and diseases might act as hindrances to our progress. Imagine closing the eyes to meditate and being flooded with thoughts of body pains. How will one be able to still the mind in this way?

Physical and breathing exercises are great for strengthening the mind, emotions, physique, and developing robust energies.

FOOD

Never consume beyond the body's limitations. Be aware of three types of food. Some foods raise stimulating thoughts and emotions, and some foods make the taste buds happy but have no positive effects on the body. Some foods, however, strengthen our physical and mental health and energy fields. You can eat the foods you enjoy, but be conscious of excess consumption that might hinder your spiritual progress.

Every person's body is different, and we need to consume foods that make the body comfortable. We have to listen to our bodies when consuming any food. The best way to do this is to sense how you feel after consuming a particular food. You need to experience it for yourself to know whether a particular food makes you energetic or exhausted. Limit foods that hinder your mental, emotional, physical, and spiritual progress.

TIPS

- Moderation and consistency are the keys to achieving good health.
- Remain consistent in exercising and maintaining personal hygiene.
- Consume and enjoy foods in moderation.

I exercise daily within an hour. It has helped me in keeping away health issues and other bodily pains that hinder spiritual progress. Make it a point to listen to your body and to develop a good sense of body awareness. I have realized that not all workouts fit a given individual's body type. Therefore, you should feel your body's needs and customize exercises to suit your body's needs through body awareness. For example, if you cannot do squats, do walking for twenty minutes daily; this helps the body grow stronger and healthier while minimizing and managing health issues, injuries, pains, and aches. The body tends to wear and tear as it ages, and it is your responsibility to respect and care for your body to minimize and eliminate its harmful effects.

THE THREE BODIES IN US

I have been talking only about the physical body in this chapter. Within ourselves, we each hold the physical body, the subtle body, and the causal body. The subtle body is your astral body, and the causal body is the body that veils the subtle and physical body. These three bodies are interconnected and hold energies that influence one another. The energies in these three bodies receive positive activation through meditation.

The physical body is the only body that is visible to the physical eye. The physical body is the one that houses, withers, and perishes.

CHAPTER 29

ENERGY CONSCIOUSNESS

MIND, EMOTION, BODY AND ENERGY influence and complement each other. To understand energy, we must look at all these parts: Mind, emotion, body, aura and chakra.

For example, the painful thoughts inside the mind generate painful negative emotions. Mental and emotional pain lead to psychosomatic symptoms. Sometimes, we will lose focus in caring for our physical health due to mental and emotional pain. When mind, emotion and body are affected, we emit a poor aura or vibe. The aura reflects our mental, emotional, and physical state. The aura also reflects the amount of cosmic positivity and light we have absorbed into our consciousness from existence.

AURA

Aura is an energy that surrounds the physical body. It is believed that there are colors in the aura and that it can be seen through deep spiritual practice. Each color represents the level of positivity and negativity surrounding the person.

An aura can be felt too. For example, when we hang around some people, we feel energized, while hanging around others might cause us to feel exhausted. Have you visited any environment that makes you feel tired? If you have experienced such feelings, you entered a place where an aura is low. Low aura in an environment means an atmosphere of sadness, poor health, negativity, and destructive energies. On the other hand, if you feel sad and enter a room filled with happy people, you will suddenly feel relaxed, calm, and relieved—the room is filled with a positive aura, and the positivity has been absorbed into you.

Chakra

Chakras play a vital role in raising positive energies in us. What is a chakra? Our body houses 72,000 nadis, 114 chakras, and 7 main chakras. Nadis and chakras are energy channels that run in our bodies. The existence communicates with us through these energy channels. Nadis are like electrical wires, chakras are like switches (power points), and the energy source that comes from existence is like the current supply. The amount of cosmic energy from existence drawn into the body determines the person's overall mental, emotional, physical, and spiritual functioning.

The supply of current cannot pass through broken electrical wires and faulty switches. In the same way, an unhealthy mind and body wouldn't be able to absorb the cosmic energy from existence. Caring for the mind and body is like ensuring that the electrical wires and switches are well placed and in good working condition to receive the current supply properly. In other words, to absorb the cosmic energy effectively in our energy systems, we need to keep our minds and bodies healthy.

ENERGY

The waves of energy that run in our body and help us in our mental, emotional, physical and spiritual functioning are called *ojas* and *tejas*. To absorb and preserve these cosmic energies, proper breathing exercise, physical exercise, healthy diet, and meditation have to be practiced. Energy is like an ocean and *ojas* and *tejas* are two kinds of waves present in that ocean.

OJAS AND TEJAS

Nadis and chakras draw energy from existence to activate these waves of energies in our body. Ojas and tejas supplement one another. An ojas is like an internal oil, and a tejas is like an internal flame. These energies coexist. The tejas is a driving force, and the ojas is a sustaining force. For example, the heat energy of the air we inhale and exhale forms tejas energy. The tejas energy then transforms into ojas energy, which nourishes, lubricates and vitalizes the body cells, chakras and aura.

So now the question is, how do nadis and chakras absorb cosmic energies from existence and then deliver them to these waves of ojas and tejas? It is through breath. Breath as the vital life force of our living is known as the prana. Breath is the transaction between us and existence. We get ourselves charged with the cosmic energy of existence through breathing exercises. These breathing exercises have the Sanskrit name pranayama.

STRENGTHENING THE ENERGIES

Let's say we want to charge our mobile phones. To charge them properly may take about an hour. If we don't charge our phones properly, we cannot use them for long periods, and if there are some malfunctions in the phone, the phone signals will never be clear. In the same way, when cosmic energies aren't absorbed properly, it affects the ojas and tejas, which in turn affect a person's overall functioning. Poor ojas and tejas cause lack of confidence, high ego, poor reasoning skills, dull physical appearance, and many other mental, emotional, and spiritual dysfunctions.

If we use our phone for unnecessary talks or waste the supply of current in our house, it will affect the phone's functioning and other electronic devices in our home. Similarly, wasting our ojas and tejas will affect our overall functioning as a person.

So what can be done to preserve these energies? In the following few chapters, I will talk about the chakras, as understanding the chakras is crucial for strengthening and preserving our energies and raising our consciousness.

POINTS TO NOTE

- Mental, emotional, and physical states affect and reflect our energy state.
- Proper physical exercise, healthy diet, breathing exercise, and meditation are needed to strengthen our energies.
- Energy in us is drawn from the cosmic energies of existence.
- Cosmic energy from existence is drawn into the nadis and chakras and permeates into our ojas and tejas.

I remain attentive to the types of energies that are radiated within and around me. I usually try to sense them through my intuition. For example, when I am with someone, I check on how I feel inside me. Energy from a person can be felt even without any verbal communication. Trust your vibes when it comes to relating to others and take care of your vibes. Keep raising your vibes, take care of them, and be aware of the vibes emitted all around us. There is a tendency to misjudge energies, especially when our minds bring along some biases and ego.

It is always good to keep our minds and bodies healthy with proper exercise, food, and meditation to build the ability to sense and safeguard energies.

Existence is created from energy; existence creates energy and communicates through energy. Ergo, preserving your sacred energy leads to exuberance.

CHAPTER 30

CHAKRAS: THE UPWARD VOYAGE

THE SEVEN CHAKRAS ARE CRITICAL and propitious points that absorb cosmic energy from existence. These cosmic energies get absorbed into the individual's body for spiritual growth. The individual will improve on his mental, emotional, physical, and spiritual functioning if the right amount of cosmic energies are absorbed into his chakras.

I will briefly share these chakra points and their unique purpose. These chakra points are the "power points" for existence to connect with us. Blocked chakra points and nadis will not support a smooth absorption of cosmic energies from existence.

What causes chakra points to be blocked?

Blockage of chakra points may be caused by deficiencies in lifestyle, habits, nutrition, rest, and exercise. In some cases, a poor sense of self-reflection, self-management, and unconscious and nonmeditative practices keep the chakras blocked.

What are the side effects of affected and blocked chakra points?

The person will remain in a metaphysical sleep. Their thoughts, emotions, communication, and actions will be unconscious and ungrounded.

Where are these chakra points located?

They are located along the spine.

What are the benefits of opening these chakra points?

Opening the chakra points facilitates self-healing, enhances intuitive powers, improves health, and makes us sharp and clear in understanding the supreme truth. Most important, it clears the path of unconsciousness and directs us towards self-realization and oneness with existence. Working on these chakra points is imperative to attain superconsciousness and cosmic consciousness. Opening and strengthening these points will bring an end to pain and suffering gradually.

CHAKRA POINTS

The works of the chakras are deep and immense. Following I will share some general works of the chakras. The points start from the base of the spine to the top.

Root chakra

Survival point.

Location: between the anus and genitals.

Purpose: represents sleep, food, and the ability to handle life situations. We call this the grounding power zone.

Signs of imbalance: negative outlook of life, psychological symptoms and ungrounded emotions. Facing eating and sleep disorders and lower limb health problems. Attachment to material things. Facing rigidity, insecurity, feeling stuck in life, overreliance on external circumstances, and fear.

Sacral chakra

Sexual point.

Location: below the navel and above the genitals.

Purpose: represents sexual energy—the procreative power zone. It is also the point of creativity, openness, and receptivity to divine connection.

Signs of imbalance: sexual issues, inability to express desires, urinary and kidney problems, struggles towards healthy self-image, lower back pain and hip mobility pain. Feeling overwhelmed with emotions or out of touch with emotions; self-esteem, guilt, and confidence issues.

Solar Plexus chakra

Gut point.

Location: solar plexus.

Purpose: represents "guts"—the willpower zone.

Signs of imbalance: fears of taking action, feeling victimized, being submissive to maintain peace, digestion problems and all stomach-related issues. A strong desire for personal power, overinflated ego, lacking the will to commit and work towards goals.

Following are the points of higher consciousness. These points hold sublime qualities.

Heart chakra

Love point.

Location: middle chest.

Purpose: represents love and compassion—the higher creativity zone. It is the point of unconditional love towards existence.

Signs of imbalance: Over-loving turns to jealousy, lack of self-compassion, inability to connect emotionally with others, causing bitter relationships and grudge-holding. Health issues related to heart, upper back, shoulder, arms and wrists, asthma, respiratory problems, and allergies.

Throat chakra

Communication point.

Location: throat.

Purpose: represents communication skills—the zone of constructive expression of thoughts and emotions.

Signs of imbalance: poor communication skills, inability to express thoughts and emotions appropriately, and a tendency to go along with others so as to not to upset anyone. Fear of expansion and growth. Health issues related to throat, jaw, ear, neck, and shoulder.

Third eye chakra

Superconsciousness point.

Location: between the eyebrows.

Purpose: known as the "seat of the divine" or the spiritual eye. It holds the tiny silvery-white star in the middle of a circle of indigo with a gold halo. This star is the point of superconsciousness. At this point, we realize "I am existence." This point is also the point of intuition. It also represents psychic abilities and intuitive powers. A strong sense of intuition is needed for communicating effectively with existence.

Signs of imbalance: Health issues related to nose, eyes, and head and lacking intuitive reasoning abilities. Imbalances here also affect communication with existence. It causes a person to be clouded with rigid intellectual conclusions and logic. It also causes a person to be ignorant about his birth and life purpose.

Crown chakra

Cosmic consciousness point.

Location: top of the head.

Purpose: to transcend into cosmic consciousness. "I am one with existence."

Signs of imbalance: rigidity, poor analysis of situations, overly attached to materials, unable to see others viewpoints, lacking aim in life, and entanglement in many unconscious actions. Opening this chakra leads to complete bliss and freedom.

My brief explanations here are just guidelines that explain the work of chakras. Suffering and pain are connected to the chakra blockages. Opening up the chakras leads to peace and liberation.

Sexual energy plays a crucial role in opening the chakras and leading one to enlightenment. When sexual energy rises up the spine instead of getting dissipated from the sexual organs, it transforms to serve a higher purpose and brings us into achieving higher possibilities. Sexual energy is a vital life force energy that helps us to raise our consciousness. Sexual energy is capable of moving in dual directions. In one direction, it can be emitted or dissipated from the body. Emission is when sexual energy is used for reproduction. Dissipating is simply wasting sexual energy through other means. For example, excessive masturbation or engaging in perverse conversation will lead to the dissipation of energies. The second direction is a transformation in which the sexual energy moves in an upward direction in the spine. When sexual energy rises up the chakras instead of leaving the body through sexual organs, it flourishes and opens all the chakras and finally arrives at the third eye and crown chakra, the gate to super and cosmic consciousness. Rising of the sexual energy in the spine is also known as the ojas energy.

It is natural for us to face blockages. My blockages have led me to suffer and go through pain. Sometimes, these blockages may drive a person into laziness and cause a person to skip spiritual practices. Mental health challenges are also related to blockages in chakras. I learned two methods to battle this: consistency and self-discipline. With consistency and self-discipline, we can put in daily efforts to open up these blocked energy channels. I will teach three meditation techniques in the following chapters that help in this transformation.

To reach to the crown chakra, we have to clear the blockages starting from the base, the root chakra, and moving in an upward direction.

Invigorate yourself with your inward flow of cosmic energies.

CHAPTER 31

POSITIVE AND NEGATIVE THINKING

WHAT ARE POSITIVE THINKING AND negative thinking, and how to apply these as a meditator? Many of us today have misconstrued the meaning of positive thinking and negative thinking. Let me explain positive and negative thinking from a meditative perspective.

Positive thinking is not merely the avoidance of a difficult situation. When applying positive thinking, we practice qualities of higher consciousness in daily life. Positive thinkers apply compassion, gratitude, courage, confidence, love, affirmation, motivation, kindness, less judgment, support, sensitivity and empathy.

Positive thinkers do away with criticizing someone, gossiping, insulting, and breaking the spirit of others. Positive thinkers lift the spirits of people. Positive thinking benefits the thinkers and the people around them. Positive thinking is abstaining from actions that jeopardize consciousness.

What is negative thinking?

Negative thinking is acting out of unconsciousness. It means thinking, feeling, communicating, and acting while being trapped in a deep metaphysical sleep. It also reflects imbalances in the chakras.

What is pseudo-positive thinking?

It is the denial of a situation, working hard to reframe a situation according to one's biases in order to feel personal relief and to avoid most life challenges. It is also about criticizing others to make oneself feel positive and good.

How may positive thinking be applied correctly?

Think about fire and electricity: both can cause harm to us, but we can transform them to good use. Fire can be used to cook and keep us warm, while electricity helps us charge our electronic devices such as laptops and mobile phones. Similarly, when a meditator encounters negativity, he can transform it positively. But transformation isn't about reframing situations according to our biases. When biases exist, it is no longer a process of positive thinking. To work towards spiritual growth, we have to clear our minds from ego and biases and use negativity as fuel to light the flame of positivity.

Nine Ways to Transform Negativity to Positivity

Here are nine great ways I learned from mystic teachers to transform negativity. These methods work great when I apply them in any adverse situations.

1. Look out for opportunities, resources, and strengths in a negative situation.
2. Be wholly present and merge with the situation. Take interest and become energized to work on the negative situations. Remember that our unconscious thoughts that wander in the past and future make a present situation appear like a huge problem. Most of the time, the problem is not a problem—it is the mind that makes a situation appear terrifying. When we give our full attention to the situation, it is no more a problem but an enjoyable challenge and lesson that grows our consciousness.
3. Practice the add and discard method. Let go of unnecessary matters that do not serve you, and add matters that will help you develop a clear perception.
4. Make a strict point of keeping your perceptions clear. Most negative things multiply in our minds due to poor perception. Clear perception means being awake, alert, and conscious.
5. Remain calm at all times. If you are not calm, your energies will start acting up anxiously or fearfully, bringing more unconsciousness into the situation.
6. Understand that a negative situation is around to raise our consciousness, and it is there to serve us benefits. Dive into the situation with full attention and courage, and you will see existence rewarding you with knowledge of taking calculated risks and delivering positive outcomes.
7. Check two directions—either you or an external party has caused the negative situation.
8. Discern between options that are within your control and areas that are beyond your control. Work smartly,

with a complete presence of mind, on areas within your control. Existence will help you to align situations to your best advantage.

9. Use wisdom to study and evaluate the situation. Let go of the negative situation if it doesn't bring you any positive results and only strengthens your ego.

NINE TYPES OF UNCONSCIOUS MOMENTS WHEN NEGATIVITY WORSENS A SITUATION

In my own life experiences, and having analyzed various challenging situations, I have concluded that these nine types of unconscious moments aggravate situations and cause more severe pains and sufferings. Be wary of these nine moments:

1. when we are working too hard to avoid or resist a challenging situation
2. suppressing and repressing thoughts, emotions, communication, and actions when dealing with the situation
3. being overly entangled with past and future thoughts while dealing with the situation
4. externalizing blame or self-blaming when dealing with the situation
5. approaching situations with maladaptive coping and dealing methods; for example, being overly dominant or submissive when dealing with situations
6. using ungrounded thoughts, emotions, and clouded perceptions to assess, evaluate, and work on the situation
7. overreliance on others to seek help on solving problems
8. applying rigid thinking patterns or repeating the same unworkable methods

9. allowing external negative situations to affect my inner spirit

TIPS

- Know the difference between positive thinking and pseudo-positive thinking.
- Apply the qualities of higher consciousness when dealing with daily life situations.
- Know the nine ways of transforming negativity to positivity.
- Know the nine types of unconscious moments.
- Meditate daily and keep a close intimate relationship with the existence.

Remain a light to yourself and be a light to others. Climbing through the ladders of self-knowledge made me realize that my darkness can nourish and embellish my light.

CHAPTER 32

SPIRITUAL BYPASSING

SPIRITUAL BYPASSING IS A TERM coined by a psychologist and Buddhist teacher named John Welwood. I love this term, and let me explain this in my own words.

Spiritual bypassing means "hiding behind spirituality." It is a way to avoid actions, embellish ego, give pseudo-sensible excuses, and mask words to bolster personal gratifications and advantages. Let me give you some examples from my life when I faced spiritual bypassing moments.

Whenever I got angry, I was advised by some acquaintances that as a meditative person I shouldn't get angry—I should learn to act and behave the "right" way. I wasn't allowed to be even assertive. I was encouraged to tolerate the wrong deeds of others and to forgive them quickly. It appalls me to hear this advice from people who are both into spiritual and nonspiritual paths. My righteous anger was told to be suppressed; my anger was seen as an unfair emotion for a meditator. A meditator who gets angry is seen as even more pessimistic than a normal person. If a meditator gets angry, some even believe that his meditation practices didn't work.

I have come across many avoidant behaviors that arise from insecurity and fear of consequences. These "no actions" are masked as being egoless, practicing spiritually to let go, or forgetting the past and forgiving. In other words, spiritual terms and words are used to elude challenges.

In other cases, spiritual words might be used to create fear in others to gain an unfair advantage. For example, "God is going to punish you, God is watching you, I will leave it to God to handle you." These words are sometimes expressions of passive aggression concealed under spirituality.

At other times, personal responsibility is negated and tied up under the guise of spirituality. For example, "I am not the reason for my problems in my life; the divine tested me, and the demon tempted me." In other circumstances, challenges and responsibilities are avoided with words such as, "Don't do anything. Leave it to God. God knows best."

There are also instances where words and information are selectively chosen, based on biases and concealed under spirituality. These types of actions reflect one's sense of unconsciousness. Therefore, spiritual bypassing is an act of unconsciousness.

It is essential to know that in spirituality, we accept both positive and negative moments. We learn to transform negativity, and we do not solely avoid everything negative. Spirituality teaches us to transform energies.

A completely avoidant person will never become a spiritual person. A spiritual person holds rebellious energies. These rebellious energies are against harmful unconscious actions within themselves and others. A spiritual person does what is morally and intuitively aligned with existence. Grounded righteous aggressions and compassion are qualities of a spiritual person. It is natural for rebellious energies to rise when encountering and dealing with unconscious situations due to the sensitivity of meditative people.

All thoughts and emotions are a natural process of humans, and no one has the right to force and change another person. A spiritual person is aware of the unconscious actions of oneself and of others. A spiritual person remains centered and wisely evaluates parts of unconsciousness that have to be addressed and intervened. This wisdom is gained and mastered through daily meditation and creating a balance between logical and intuitive reasoning.

For example, if we meet a rude person who uses harsh words to hurt our sense of self-respect, we need to safeguard our self-respect and peace with assertive communication and actions. It's not wise to completely avoid such situations and be unfairly taken advantage of in the name of spirituality.

However, if person behave passively by not answering our calls or using less impacting words, such as "I won't friend you" or "Please don't call me anymore!" These words sound less harmful to our self-respect. You may choose to let go of problems that doesn't really bother your self-respect or spiritual development.

Again, meditation teaches you inner wisdom on what behaviors and actions must be attended to, acknowledged, or avoided. Meditation teaches you to be rebellious with righteous grounded aggression towards harmful unconscious behaviors. Meditation also preserves your energy by helping you to pick your battles. In some acts of unconsciousness, you may have to proceed with compassion rather than assertiveness.

Some spiritual bypassers gather evidence from books to give spiritual excuses for their preferred ego-driven and biased actions. When it comes to reading spiritual books, I would say it is always good to read them after meditation with a clear state of mind to absorb the contents without clouded perceptions.

Spiritual bypassing affects the mental, emotional, and spiritual health of a person. We must remain conscious of such spiritual bypassing in daily life. For example, if someone commits a guilty act, never scare them by tying their guilt with spirituality. Spirituality is not about scaring a person; it is about helping a person transcend guilt and create a sense of inner balance.

Spirituality is not about always being perfectly good or avoiding the bad. It's is about being aware of both, centering oneself, and ultimately overcoming the good and the bad. Spirituality is about being conscious and acting consciously.

In spirituality, I learn from every moment and apply what fits my personal spiritual growth. I work on being aware of my unconsciousness. I never allow the unconsciousness in others to affect my spirit. I work on becoming free of judgments and impositions.

CHAPTER 33

CHAKRA MEDITATION

IN THE FOLLOWING CHAPTERS ABOUT meditation, I will cover simple exercises to prepare the body for meditation and provide guided meditations. I have tried these meditations, and they have worked great in raising wakefulness, alertness, awareness, and consciousness.

To do meditation, sit down with your legs crossed and keep the spine straight. As the energies move upwards in the spine from the root chakra to the crown chakra, it is imperative to sit upright to allow the energy to travel upwards at ease.

The whole body has to be healthy and robust, especially the back, hip flexors, and lower limbs. If you have back problems, it is good to rest your body against a wall when meditating to give you some form of back support. Then as you gradually pick up strength, you can start doing meditations without resting your back on the wall.

SEVEN BASIC EXERCISES

Here are seven basic floor exercises that could be done to strengthen the full body for supporting meditation. These workouts are easy and can be completed within fifteen minutes in the comfort of your home. You do not need any equipment and can go at your own pace. These exercises are able to warm up and energize the chakra points.

1. push-ups for the heart chakra and spine
2. superman floor exercise or cobra yoga pose for the heart, throat, sacral, and solar plexus chakras and spine
3. squats for the root, sacral, and solar plexus chakras and spine
4. planks for the sacral, solar plexus, and heart chakras and spine
5. Neck rotations, arm circles or add in any comfortable stretching movements of your choice for the head, neck, arms, and other body parts to relieve tightness, increase flexibility, and improve blood circulation
6. downward dog yoga pose for all chakra points
7. warrior yoga pose one and two for all chakra points

I find the cobra, downward dog and warrior yoga poses great for achieving an overall body stretch before and after meditation. You are free to add in any exercises that will help you to attain a healthy and flexible physique. It is best to listen to your body and use your intuition when it comes to selecting and doing workouts to avoid injuries.

Purpose of Stretching

You can stretch your body before meditating if you feel that you need to loosen up some tightness. This increased flexibility helps you to achieve a calm and peaceful mind when meditating.

Tightness in the body is similar to rigidity in mind. Loosening up and relaxing your muscles help you to remain calm and less fidgety during meditation.

Yoga movements are also great to align our energies with existence. It is good to learn and practice them with a trained spiritual coach.

Any form of exercise is adequate to keep the body healthy, energetic, and robust. The purpose of these exercises isn't to prepare us for a show, contest, or competition—it is to attain a healthy and spiritually fit body that helps us in raising our consciousness.

FOODS

Examples of foods that help with meditation are nuts, fruits, vegetables, seeds, millet, whole grains, honey, and milk. In my experience, lemons, neem and turmeric have excellent effects in meditation. These types of foods are *pranic foods*—that is, they help the prana (breath and vital energies of the body). They support the initiation, transformation and preservation of energies for positive and constructive use.

Listen to your body when it comes to the consumption of foods. For example, alcohol is a non-pranic food. It distorts consciousness and is never helpful when it comes to meditation. Meat raises desires and sexual energy. This form of sexual energy activation from meat might drive a person to release sexual energies out of the body rather than transforming these energies inwardly for higher purposes. When it comes to food, you need to use your intuition, experiment for yourself and check on how you feel mentally, emotionally, and physically upon consumption.

RAJAS, TAMAS AND SATTVA NATURE

In Yogi philosophy, there are three kinds of nature in man. They are the *rajas, tamas and sattva* nature. The rajas nature is activated by eating stimulating foods such as caffeine and meat. It heightens the energy level. For example, rajasic foods causes overstimulation, excitement, anger, lust, or anxiety. The tamas nature is activated by consuming alcohol and high starchy foods. Tamasic foods make you sluggish, sleepy and lethargic. Sattvic foods include seeds, millet, neem, turmeric, whole wheat, fruits, vegetables, and nuts. Sattvic foods help you keep your mind, emotions, body, and energies stable and calm, and increase your intelligence. Sattvic diet also means that you choose foods wisely and consume them in moderation, which are ideal for your body's well-being. Sattvic foods are excellent for meditation.

CHAKRA MEDITATION

Here are three steps to chakra meditation:

1. **Grounding.** Do five to ten rounds of conscious(mindful) inhalation and exhalation of breath to help cleanse the nadis. Cleansing nadis means making the energy channels or pathways clear for the cosmic energy to travel smoothly to the chakra points.
2. **Attention.** Close your eyes and visualize. Go to each point of the seven chakras and place your attention on each point.
3. **Visualization.** Visualize light energy shining brightly on these chakra points.

THREE WAYS TO VISUALIZE

I will use throat and sacral chakras as examples of ways to visualize.

Spine visualization. Instead of placing attention on the body part, you can place your attention on the spine area which horizontally corresponds to the body part of your chakra. For example, place your attention directly at the back of your neck (spine area) to visualize the throat chakra. Similarly, you can place your attention at the lower back (spine area) to visualize the sacral chakra which is below the navel and above the genitals.

Body part visualization. You can place your attention on the point below the navel for sacral chakra or directly on your throat for throat chakra instead of focusing on spine areas.

Simultaneous visualization. Place your attention on both the spine and the body part at the same time. For example, you can imagine the light energy glowing simultaneously at your throat and back of your neck, or glowing at the lower back and below the navel.

LIGHT COLORS FOR THE CHAKRAS

You can visualize these colors glowing at the chakra points.

root	red
sacral	orange
solar	yellow
heart	green
throat	blue
third eye	indigo
crown	white

Alternatively, you can also visualize a golden or white light for every chakra point.

Always start from the root chakra and end at the crown chakra. For the root chakra, you have to focus on the point between the genitals and the anus. You have to pass from one chakra to the other in an upward direction until you reach the crown chakra. For the third eye chakra, you can visualize the light at the back of your head, at the center of the eyebrow, or both. You have to place your attention on the top of your head for the crown chakra.

Place your attention on the chakra points and visualize the light shining brightly on the chakra points. Feel the warmness of this light for as long as you want, and slowly move up from one chakra point to the next.

You have completed one cycle when you start from the root and reach the crown chakra. You can repeat the cycle as many times as you wish. For beginners, one to two cycles will be good. This meditation can be done twice a day, morning and evening.

Once you have completed the meditation, you can thank the existence and ask for its protection and inner guidance to guide and lead you towards self-realization, and then you can open your eyes.

In my experience of chakra meditation, I came to understand my areas of blockages. I was able to clear these blockages with physical interventions like changing lifestyle, eating habits, and exercise. If you have been alerted by existence to seek medical treatment, then do seek attention immediately. For example, in some cases, with regular practice chakra meditation clears back pain with its healing light. In other cases, chakra meditation will give you intuitive insight into taking physical (medical) interventions to heal your blockages. Spiritual messages from existence vary according to individual cosmic energies, life situation, health condition, and years of meditative practice.

CHAPTER 34

WATCHER MEDITATION

In watcher meditation, you simply close your eyes and watch. Just watch the thought, watch the breath, and watch anything that happens within you. You have to walk along with your mind and watch the points where your mind arrives. But do remember that you need to keep a distance when you watch. You need to be very alert about not merging and entangling yourself with your thought.

When thoughts wander and move in all directions, remain watching them without getting entangled. The mind suddenly will reach a point where it has to rest. It is during this rest that you arrive at the present moment. As the mind enters the present moment, it stops swaying to the past and future. Bringing the mind into the present moment is called *stilling the mind*. In stillness, thoughts cease gradually, and then the meditator will transcend into a thoughtless space. From the thoughtless space, he will transcend into superconsciousness and cosmic consciousness. However, transcending to thoughtless, super, and cosmic consciousness requires lots of patience and consistent meditation practice.

During watcher meditation, you will come across many thoughts. You can see these thoughts as guests who visit your home. These guests come and leave; you do not hold onto them and get yourself entangled with them. In watcher meditation, you remain a host who witnesses thoughts *from a distance*, without being disturbed and affected.

Before doing watcher meditation, you can do the same breathing exercises, physical exercises, and stretches mentioned in the chakra meditation. Here are five steps to remember before doing the watcher meditation.

1. Sit down in a comfortable place and close your eyes.
2. Tell yourself that you will keep a distance between yourself, your mind, and your body. That means you remain entirely as a separate person from your mind and body.
3. Tell yourself that you are neither the thought nor the emotion that arises in you when you are meditating. You remain as a host or witness who watches without participating. You need to tell yourself to be aware that you are not the participant but only the watcher.
4. Now remain in this state as a watcher as you pay attention to the activities of your mind.
5. If your thoughts try to entangle you, immediately become aware and gently create a distance and resume being the watcher. Do not struggle, fight, or resist the thought. Gently separate yourself from being the participant of your thought (let go of any thought that tries to hold you tightly), create a distance, and become the watcher again.

How I Practice Watcher Meditation

Here is an example of how I practice watcher meditation. As I close my eyes to meditate, I enter into a void where I keep myself distant from my thoughts, emotions, and body. As my thoughts drift in, I watch each of them without getting entangled. As I hear a noise, I pay attention to it without getting entangled, and as I feel a tingling on my skin, I pay attention to it without getting entangled. I move with my thought while keeping a distance between myself and my thought. As my mind slowly settles for rest, thoughts slowly cease, and gradually I enter a state of stillness and slowly enter a space of no-mind.

You can also experience this space in the gaps between your thoughts. For example, when moving from one thought to the next, you will experience a moment of emptiness. This emptiness is the state of no-mind. It may seem empty, but these empty points hold blessings and positive vibrations of the existence that prepares you for liberation.

For example, when you watch a movie on TV, you watch it without becoming the actor or actress in the movie. You watch the movie from a distance while sitting on your sofa. Similarly, in watcher meditation, you observe from a distance your thoughts, feelings, and sensations that are happening within and around you.

Points to Remember about Meditation

There are no wholly fixed methods to perform meditations. Three things to know when doing meditation is to make the effort, keep ourselves as conscious as possible while doing it, and remain consistent in doing meditation daily. The existence is merciful and will accept our efforts, forgive our mistakes, and gradually reward us. We have to put our complete trust in existence when engaging in meditations.

After completing the meditation, we can express our gratitude and ask for protection and inner guidance from the existence.

CHAPTER 35

CENTERING MEDITATION

THIS MEDITATION IS WHAT I call centering meditation. You can start this meditation by doing the same light physical exercises and stretches, together with some conscious breath inhalations and exhalations taught in the previous chapters. Here are three steps for centering meditation.

BEGINNER PHASE: FIX YOUR ATTENTION TO A POINT ON YOUR BODY

1. Sit in a comfortable position, with your legs crossed and spine straight.
2. Close your eyes and place your attention on any specific point on your body. For example, you can place it on one of your fingers, toes, shoulders, or chest points. The most common centering points used in meditations are navel (sacral chakra), middle chest (heart), and the middle of the eyebrows.
3. As your mind wanders, become aware and bring your attention back to this specific point on your body part. Continue keeping your attention fixed on this point.

Two key points:

- No matter where you keep your attention fixed, you will gradually drift into the third eye point at mid eyebrow.
- Your energy flows into the points where you keep your attention; this meditation method also helps in healing the body parts.

What do I do if my centering point suddenly changes?

When you gradually move into the middle of your eyebrows while meditating on any other body points, do not panic or work hard to go back to your first point. Remain relaxed when you reach mid eyebrow and hang in there.

Can I start directly at the middle of my eyebrows (third eye)?

Yes, you can start directly at mid eyebrow. When meditating, you do not have to strain your eyes. Close your eyes and calmly place your attention at the midpoint of your eyebrows in a completely relaxed manner.

Why are the middle of the eyebrows, the middle of the chest, and the navel the best centering points?

The middle of the eyebrows is the house of the third eye. It is the home of superconsciousness. You may get some psychic energies kicking in when meditating, but that is not superconsciousness. You may also experience satori, glimpses of light (mini enlightenments). It would be best to continue with consistent practice to enter into a state of superconsciousness; this requires patience and consistent practice. Also, keep in mind that though we call the midpoint of the eyebrows the third eye, the third eye is not precisely seated at mid eyebrow. The middle of the eyebrows is the guiding path or doorstep to enter into the spiritual eye, which is deep inside us. The third eye or spiritual eye is the subtle or astral eye that lies beyond the physical dimension.

The navel is the starting point where sexual energies are highly active. It is a chakra point for procreation. Placing your attention here helps activate these sexual energies to rise from the spine towards the midpoint of the eyebrows (third eye chakra) and top of the head (crown chakra). Sexual energy is spiritual energy. The middle of the chest (heart chakra) is the beginning point for the state of higher consciousness.

Centering meditation can be used to activate chakra points. Alternatively, if you want to energize any of your chakra points, you can pay attention to the chakra point and keep your attention fixed at this point. For example, if you need to improve your sense of self-compassion, you can keep your attention on the heart point. And of course, you will gradually transcend into the middle of the eyebrows.

Intermediate Phase: Bringing in Breath to the Point of Attention

To make your meditations more exciting and joyful, you can start watching your breath essence in these centering points.

Here is how I do it. I keep my attention on my navel and watch my breath moving up and down at my belly center. Similarly, I can watch and feel my breath moving in and out, or rising up and down on the third-eye center between the eyebrows. When I say that I "watch" my breath essence, I am saying that I remain aware of the movement of my breath on the body part or point of attention.

Advanced Phase: Bringing in Breath and Light

You can visualize the light color of your chakra if you are using the chakra point for centering meditation. For example, if I want to focus on my navel point, I will visualize orange or gold/white light. I keep my attention centered or fixed to this navel point and visualize orange/gold/white light; simultaneously, I watch my breath essence—I am aware of my breath movements at this navel point.

I am doing three things together: attention on that point (stillness), visualization of light on that point (healing), and awareness of breath movement on that point (bringing myself into the present moment, energizing myself and working towards superconsciousness with breath work).

Breathing exercises (pranayama) provides vital prana energy. This prana energy charges the body with cosmic energies of existence.

Another example of the advanced practice: I place my attention on my chest (heart chakra). I visualize a green/gold/white light shining brightly on the middle of my chest and watch my chest rising up and down as it is filled with breath essence (inhalation and exhalation of breath). I hold my attention in this process of meditation. If any thoughts come by, I become aware and let go of those thoughts and continue bringing my attention back to the meditative process.

What if I want to place my attention on other parts of my body other than the seven chakras?

Yes, you can do that. You can visualize a light (white or gold) on any body part.

Does this centering meditation help in healing?

Yes, it helps you in the meditation and also in the healing process of the body part. But healing doesn't happen overnight; it happens through consistent practice, faith, and gratitude—the seeds of consciousness. You can add in affirmations such as, "Dear existence, I am healing in your divine grace."

Healing has many deep and differing methods. I am just sharing the essentials here. These methods heal not only your physical parts but also your psychological and emotional states. For example, paying attention to navel points helps heal digestive issues, lower back pain, sexual dysfunction, and self-esteem and confidence issues.

Here is an example of how spiritual healing is done step by step with centering meditation:

1. Inhale and exhale five to ten times consciously; this clears your mind and connects you with the cosmic energies of existence.
2. Do the chakra or centering meditation. Place attention, visualize light color or light energy, and watch breath movements on the chakra point or body part that needs healing energies.
3. Say your affirmation: "Dear Existence, I am healing well. I am healing fine, and I will heal to become better in your divine grace."
4. Thank existence and open your eyes.

Do this daily and have faith and trust in the miracles of existence. Do see your doctor simultaneously while doing this if you want to heal fast. Keep in mind that spiritual healing takes time.

It is good to start practicing the beginner methods and start trying those intermediate and advanced ones later. I find these methods helpful for stilling the mind, raising self-awareness, healing and strengthening intuition and clairvoyance.

Overall Benefits

Centering meditation makes me more attentive and alert. Moreover, I find it more exciting to modify and spice up my meditation sessions using breath watching and light visualizing techniques at these points. The more alert and attentive I am at these centering points, the more I am able to remain still and keep my thoughts from wandering. The existence grants immense blessing during these moments of silence. It transforms the meditator into an imperturbable person with improved intuitive reasoning skills and clairvoyance.

Centering meditation helps us to be in balance. We develop an unassailable spirit and remain in harmony within ourselves. It raises our ability to fathom situations and know the perceptible and imperceptible factors embedded in them. This meditation strengthens our spiritual ability to self-reflect incisively and respond with intelligence.

After the meditation is over, you may open your eyes and express your gratitude to the existence and seek blessings, protection, and guidance.

Meditations can be done for any length of time, from a minute to an hour. A minute of meditation a day is still better than no meditation.

Are there other ways to do meditation if I don't have the time?

Yes, simply be aware and conscious of your day-to-day activities. Any action done with complete awareness and consciously is meditation. Any conscious action that brings your mind to the present moment is a meditation method.

Meditation isn't just an activity that is wholly done in a seated position for a specific time. Meditation should gradually move into our day-to-day activities. Meditation in its euphoric and unfeigned meaning is a state of thoughtlessness, superconsciousness, and cosmic consciousness.

CHAPTER 36

Cosmic Romantic Moments with Existence

Life is not all about suffering and pain. Your intuition speaks to you. Upon reading this book, starting with the preface, you will be able to conclude the purpose of your life. As you read this book, existence should have spoken within you what you need to make your life peaceful, blissful, and meaningful.

My insight is that it is good to understand two important purposes of life: to develop a cosmic union with existence through self-realization, and to serve and contribute to existence in order to create a sense of meaning for ourselves and others.

Cosmic union is attained through meditations and spiritual practices. Cosmic union is about knowing about ourselves, which involves growing your consciousness and healing parts of us that cause us suffering. The other purpose is to create a sense of meaning for our lives so that we can perform our daily duties with responsibility.

Our daily duties are like earning credibility points in the existence's records system. Our dedication towards our duties will be reciprocated with material success from existence.

Though material success isn't compelling in bringing us towards higher consciousness, it is still helpful to keep us at peace and away from poverty. Our minds will be calmer if our living conditions are good and peaceful and we don't have to fight because materials are inadequate. Fewer struggles mean less-painful thoughts, which indirectly help us to work towards liberation. Most humans desire and strive for a happy, successful, and affluent life, don't they?

Some believe that we have to renounce material progress to be spiritually successful. I learned that material success is never an encumbrance for a spiritual man; spiritual renunciation should take place from within. For example, spiritual renunciation means I let go of any activities that stops me from rising spiritually. If material success is massaging the unhealthy parts of one's ego, then it might hinder spiritual development.

From my experience and knowledge from mystic teachings, I learned ten great ways to create a harmonious spiritual life and enjoy material successes awarded by existence. I call these ten ways as *cosmic romantic moments*, as they help us progressively reach higher states of consciousness. I practiced them, and it worked. Hence, I am sharing them with you.

1. Practice Conscious Actions and Concurrent Reflections

We should practice being conscious of our actions and practice doing concurrent reflections; this means being watchful over our thoughts, emotions, communication, and actions from moment to moment. If you realize that your actions run into unconscious directions, ask yourself questions immediately as to why you think, feel, communicate, and act this way.

Most times, it is challenging to be completely conscious of every action. Therefore, we should incorporate concurrent reflections in our daily life activities. Concurrent reflections are great ways to reset the mind, and they bring us back into the present state of mind if our minds wander into unconscious directions. Concurrent reflections are reflections done immediately after an occurrence of thought, emotion, communication, or action. The more present we are, the more conscious we become. Conscious actions lead us to higher consciousness and bring in a more qualitative state of living. Existence sends positive vibrations that work in our favor when we are conscious.

2. **Honesty**

Honesty is one of the master keys for opening spiritual doors. When we are working towards understanding ourselves and raising our consciousness, we need to be brutally honest with ourselves. Being honest to ourselves means realizing our metaphysical sleep and accepting that we have dark sides. Honesty is practiced after eliminating ego-based reasoning. Fighting, resisting, and denying the truth will only multiply pains and suffering. Be very aware of how the ego plays a dangerous role in hindering us from seeing or accepting the truth about ourselves. Be ready to admit to yourself how your unconsciousness is taking a toll on your life. Find your dark shadows, admit them to yourself, and heal yourself by clearing them. Leave your ego aside when doing honest reflections. Existence will help you to heal and will bring you to greater heights of consciousness in this way.

3. **Daily Decrease**

Decrease the existing factors that contribute to metaphysical sleep. For example, remove one harmful habit a day. We should also be aware of spilling our pains and suffering onto others. We should build the capability to manage what is happening inside us without causing misery to others. Limit small talks and the company of those who drag you into their hell of unconsciousness, and limit indulging in habits and activities that jeopardize your consciousness. *You need to raise your inner light by lowering the darkness within and around you.*

4. **Daily Increase**

   Increase the qualities of higher consciousness in you; for example, practice compassion, love, faith, trust and sensitivity. Increase the time you spend with highly conscious and self-realized people. Read and watch content that grows your consciousness—reading this book is one way of raising your consciousness. *You need to walk closer each day to the light of existence.*

5. **Contributing Always**

   Contribute to the existence and humanity. "What you give to me, I will return to you," is the existence's style of communicating with us. If we contribute positively to the wellness of existence, the existence will reciprocate with an abundance of goodness and positivity in our own lives.

6. **Safeguarding**

   Make a serious point of safeguarding your mental, emotional, physical, and spiritual space and development. You should be wary and conscious of what comes into your life and what leaves your life. It can be any food, persons, content, situation, or environment. Ask yourself whether they are here to serve you and lift you in your spiritual progress, or whether they are around to cause more pains and suffering. If something takes a toll on your peace and spiritual development, you need to let it go. *Existence helps you if you help yourself.*

7. Doing Positive Things Avidly

Bring yourself into a mindset where you avidly do gratitude prayers, exercise, meditate, read, write, and eat healthy food. The secret behind self-realization and achieving success is to do avidly what we do; this brings us into the flow state and makes us present. We must take the interest and initiative to work on our tasks daily; we should love and enjoy doing things that contribute positivity to our lives. To maintain personal hygiene, you cannot skip a day without brushing your teeth. Similarly, if you want to be in union with existence, you cannot neglect your health, daily meditations, and conscious actions.

8. Enjoying Life Lessons

Enjoy receiving fresh lessons from existence. Be it good or challenging moments, all of them are simply lessons to raise our consciousness. Build the courage to love the unknown. Take a courageous dive into the ocean of life, and swim with unconditional love and trust in existence; existence will gradually guide you into an island of cosmic consciousness. When suffering and pains arise, never feel disheartened. See suffering and pains as wake-up calls to raise your consciousness and gradually heal. Daily learning and daily healing are essential processes for self-realization.

9. Keeping Mind, Body, and Heart in Harmony

Keep your intellect, intuition, and instincts in harmony. Intellect is our mind's information and knowledge. Intuition (heart) is the bridge between us and existence. Instincts are bodily responses. Intuition grows through meditation. As intuition grows, keep it aligned and in harmony with the mind and body; this raises clairvoyance, intelligence, and consciousness. When mind, heart, and body are not in harmony, it leads a person towards acts of unconsciousness. Your mind, body, and heart should be in harmony to keep yourself aligned with the cosmic energies of existence.

10. Daily Meditation

Even five minutes of your time devoted to meditation will reap positive results for you. You can start doing five minutes of meditation upon waking up and before going to bed. Gradually, you can increase your time. The more you meditate, the deeper your intimate relationship with existence grows. Meditate and then continue with your daily duties. Meditation centers a person and supports one in the qualitative functioning of life peripheries. It raises awareness about our ego, and controls and restrains flaunting actions that beseech ego validations; this smoothens spiritual progression.

I hope this book has helped open up new insights as we search for spiritual answers from existence and work towards knowing about ourselves. You can reread these chapters if you need to activate some inner guidance.

Existence communicates in different ways to different people, and our spiritual progress varies according to our individual spiritual practices. Nevertheless, I believe this book would be an excellent personal spiritual guide to anyone with the fervent will to seek the truth, build deep connections with existence, and work on liberation.

Thank you for reading the cosmic insights. All the best for your journey towards self-realization.

CPSIA information can be obtained
at www.ICGtesting.com
Printed in the USA
LVHW110053200422
716647LV00003B/13

9 781482 879377